John !

Sharon Weiser

What Is The *Vine* Producing?

Discover What Makes a More Fruitful Life

Sharon Weisser

WESTBOW
PRESS®
A DIVISION OF THOMAS NELSON
& ZONDERVAN

WestBow Press books may be ordered through booksellers or by contacting:

WestBow Press
A Division of Thomas Nelson & Zondervan
1663 Liberty Drive
Bloomington, IN 47403
www.westbowpress.com
1 (866) 928-1240

ISBN: 978-1-5127-2256-7 (sc)
ISBN: 978-1-5127-2257-4 (e)

Library of Congress Control Number: 2015920115

Print information available on the last page.

WestBow Press rev. date: 12/11/2015

Contents

Introduction

In God's Word we find numerous references to vineyards, vines and various fruits. Although these are sometimes used in the literal sense, they are more often used symbolically. In the Old Testament God compared Israel to a vineyard or vine which was to be used as the Root for the birth of Christ the Messiah. In the New Testament Jesus Himself taught several parables using the symbols of vineyards, vines, branches and grapes. In John 15 Jesus explained that He was the Vine and we as Christians are branches created to bear fruit. In this book we will look at these Biblical illustrations to examine our fruitfulness. Are we bearing fruit and if so what kind of fruit? We need to produce profitable and attractive fruit. Just as the vinekeeper appraises the vine by the appearance and quality of the fruit of its branches, so the world rates the value and authenticity of Christ, the True Vine, by the fruit of His branches. Hopefully in this writing we will be challenged to honestly evaluate our own fruitfulness and to learn some practical lessons in how to be more fruitful and live the abundant, overflowing life which brings others to the Vine.

"I came that they may have and enjoy life,
and have it in abundance (to the full, till
it OVERFLOWS)"

Jesus
Recorded in John 10:10
Amplified Bible

This book is dedicated to my sister Pat who was always here
to support and help me and to Debbie Hock who allowed
God to work through her, not only to show me how much
God loved me, but used her to mentor me in my Christian life.

Foreword

When I was a junior at Messiah College I had a course entitled Major Prophets taught by C.N. Hostetter, who was not only the college president at that time, but a wonderful and mature man of God. When we reached the fifth chapter of Isaiah he taught about the unfruitful vineyard and God's disappointment with Israel's lack of fruit. I have never been able to forget it. For many years since, that parable has been special to me. Along with this parable I have studied Jesus' parable usually referred to as the Wicked Husbandmen. It finally led me into the study of the symbolic and literal mention of vineyards and grapes throughout the Old and New Testaments. The use of this symbolism taught me a lot about the Christian life with references to vines producing wild grapes, sour grapes, bitter grapes and even no grapes at all. This book is a result of this study and hopefully as I share my thoughts, God will speak to you as He did to me and challenge us to produce valuable fruit. True of all parables, there are limitations to the use of symbols. Please excuse any of my inconsistencies or overuse of them.

(All Scripture quoted is from the King James
Version unless otherwise designated.)

Chapter 1

God Gives Me a Grapevine

A few years ago my sister and I bought a house together. Actually she did more buying than I did because she has had a "real" job all of her life and I have spent most of my life in missions and Christian education and the kind of job in which you don't get a "real" paycheck.

Neither of us has had the fortune (or misfortune?) of marrying and have lived in different states and/or countries since I graduated from college. Although for years we had been apart (from a few hundred to a few thousand miles) we were finally only about three hours away from each other. I was teaching at a private Christian school in Pennsylvania and my sister was working at her "real" job in New Jersey. When we would get together during breaks from school, she and I would talk about the fact that we both would soon be retiring and should think about living together. She figured she would retire first and would move to Pennsylvania and we could buy a home together. We talked about where we would like to purchase a lot and what kind of a house we would like to build. We each had our list of what the house should have to meet our individual likes and wants.

One day on my way to school I passed a particular house, as I usually did, that was owned by an older couple that had worked at the school where I was teaching. They had built this house on property right next to the school because they had helped out with janitorial work at school. This particular morning I heard the Lord speak to me and say that someday I was going to live in that house. I had driven past that house hundreds of times on my way to school and

1

had never really thought about buying it. It was a nice house, but I was not thinking of buying a house already built. When this came to me "out of the blue," I immediately dismissed it as my imagination. The possibility of ever living there was ridiculous because I would never be able to afford it. The thought was a fleeting one because I soon had my mind on what I needed to do at school that day. A few weeks later that same thought came to me as I drove by. This time I thanked the Lord and told Him I received it if it truly came from Him. God had always proved faithful in the past to supply housing for me when I needed it. It had always come just in time and at a price I could afford. However my mind reasoned that this house would never be for sale, since this couple had a lot of family who might eventually want it and even if it were put on the market, it would be far beyond my budget.

About a year later as I was going to school on a Friday morning I saw a "For Sale" sign in front of this house. My heart began to beat fast. MY house was being sold. The timing didn't seem right. My sister had just retired a few months before and was working part time for her church and still living in her own home in New Jersey. I also had just bought and moved into a secondhand trailer a few months before this. My sister had given me money for the down payment and I had a monthly mortgage payment. I had never shared with anyone, not even my sister, what I thought the Lord had told me. She was still thinking about building a new house. However I called the real estate dealer who had helped me purchase my trailer and she told me the house was very nice and being sold at a very reasonable price, because they were eager to sell in order to move into a retirement village. She advised me to call my sister immediately because it would not be on the market long. My sister arranged to come from New Jersey the next day to look at the house. With our want list in mind, we went through the house. It was unbelievable. The house had every feature that each of us had in mind plus many other features we liked but had not even thought about or planned to have. Within a few weeks it was ours. It was as if the house had been built with us in mind. After we started moving into it we realized not only did the house suit our needs and wishes, but the yard was more to our liking than we had imagined or realized at first. It contained so many trees, plants, and shrubs we had enjoyed in our yard where we had grown up- apple trees, rhubarb, flowers and a concord grapevine! God knew all this long before we did and had planned for us to own it and enjoy it one day.

The promise of God to the Israelites came to my mind:

> "And it shall be when the Lord thy God shall have brought thee into the land which he sware to give thee great and goodly cities, which thou buildest not, and houses full of all good things ...and wells digged which thou diggedst not, vineyards and olive tree, which thou plantedst not; when thou shalt have eaten and be full; then beware lest thou forget the Lord which brought thee forth..." (Deut. 6:10-12)

This seemed to be God's promise fulfilled for us. We not only had city water in the house but a well for watering the yard and gardens. The back door lock and key had the brand name "Weiser" and although we spell our name "Weisser" it seemed like God was reminding us that He was the one that had it all planned.

One of the blessings was the concord grapevine on a trellis in the backyard. Purple concord grapes were a favorite of ours and had been the kind we grew at our childhood home. We were looking forward to eating our homegrown grapes and hopefully canning juice for the winter. Our first summer I watched the vines produce leaves and small bunches of green grapes however by summer the grapes had all dried up and fallen to the ground. There were no grapes. I looked back to my childhood and tried to remember what we had done to our vines to get such sweet grapes but could not think of anything. I pruned them in February, tried to be more diligent in watering the vine and even put some fertilizer on the ground near the roots. The second summer there were only a few small bunches to enjoy. I was very disappointed but knew that I lacked the needed skill to grow grapes. Over the next few years I learned a great deal about grapes and grapevines from my friend Debbie. With her help and advice I have been able to enjoy fresh grapes and delicious grape juice during the winter months.

Through this experience I learned some new things from the Lord. He reminded me of Isaiah 5. As I did more research and study in God's

Word I found there are many references to grapes and vineyards in Scripture. God illustrates spiritual lessons using vineyards and grapes. We can find grapes that are wild, sour, and even poisonous.

This study has revealed a number of spiritual truths to me. God has challenged me to examine myself to see if I am producing good attractive and "palatable" fruit for His use and glory. During this study God revealed the connection between the Old Testament grapevine illustration in Isaiah 5 and the New Testament parable told by Jesus in the Gospels. I understand now that in each of these parables there was fruitlessness and that there were no edible grapes.

Think about it

1. Can you think of a time that God showed you something and how it took time until God performed it? If you are reading this book with others share answers to prayer and encourage each other to have faith in God.

Chapter 2

God Created the World to be Fruitful

Before the days of home freezers, my mother canned fruits and vegetables most of the summer on into early fall. As I look back it seems to me that we spent the majority of the hot summer days in the garden picking crops or in the kitchen canning them. I will admit it was a wonderful feeling in the fall to be able to go down to the cellar and see the long shelves lined with bottles of corn, beans, carrots, beets, peaches, pears, plums, pickles, jellies and jams and juices of all sorts. However I did not enjoy the work that had to be done to get the shelves full. It was hard work picking peas, beans, berries, etc. from our huge garden, only to be followed by sitting in a hot kitchen (no home air conditioning either) washing, peeling, cutting and packing fresh produce into jars. We even made our own sauerkraut and pickles which were stored in crocks. Some of these foods were less desirable than others, like carrots and pears. They always seemed to take the most work! Besides that I did not enjoy sampling them while working!

Grapes were one of the last crops put away for winter. They were made into jelly or juice. The grapes were usually harvested in our area of New York after the first frost, so the weather was cooler and so was the kitchen. The other nice thing to me as a child was that my grandparents and mother did most of the work, because we kids were back in school. Also grapes were one of the more pleasant tasting fruits. They seemed to me to be one of God's more tasty creations.

We read in Genesis that after God created each part of His whole original universe that He said- "it was good." After He created the vegetation He commanded it to bring forth "after his kind" The animals, plants and man himself were told to be fruitful. At the end of the sixth day after God had created man we find these words- "... God saw every thing that He had made, and, behold it was **very good**."

Although we do not read by name all the vegetation created, it is most likely God created grapes as one of the fruits to be enjoyed by Adam and Eve in the Garden of Eden when He spoke the variety of vegetation into existence on the third day of creation.

There is no Biblical verse to prove that grapevines were created at that time, but we do know that grapes are one of the oldest known fruits. According to the World Book Encyclopedia, fossils of grape leaves and grape seeds have been found and dated as "prehistoric". Paintings of vineyards and grapes which have been dated as far back as 2440 B.C. have been found on Egyptian tombs

The word "grapes" is not found in Scripture until Genesis 40 in the account of Joseph in prison, when he interpreted the dream of the chief butler of Pharaoh. The butler dreamed he was giving grapes to Pharaoh. Joseph told him that meant that he would be restored to his former position in Potiphar's household. However in Genesis 9:20 we do find that the word "vineyard' is mentioned in connection with Noah. We read that Noah cultivated the ground and planted a vineyard. Without showing a time sequence we discover in the very next verse that he drank of the wine "...and was drunken" Therefore we can conclude Noah either took shoots of grapevines or grape seeds with him on the ark or that the vines withstood the waters.

It is tragic that the first mention of the existence of grapes is seen in the misuse of wine. The results of Noah's drunkenness ended in a curse upon Ham. Drunkenness and its consequences are still a tragedy in today's society. It has resulted in generational curses. Thank God that Jesus' death and resurrection can break this curse!

Another misuse of wine leading to sin is mentioned in Genesis 19:36-38. After Lot escaped from the city of Sodom, his daughters, afraid they would never have husbands or children, got him drunk and slept with him. The result of this action was the birth of two sons, Moab and Benammi, whose descendants were enemies of the children of Israel for many generations. The Moabites refused passage to Israel on Israel's way to Canaan. (Num. 21:13-15) They also tried to get Balaam to curse Israel. (Num. 22 – 24) Yet it is interesting to note that Ruth, a Moabitess accepted the God of Israel and is one of two women mentioned in the chronological Messianic line through Joseph. (Matt. 1:5)

Wine was used as part of the ceremonial worship of Israel. The priests were to have a continual offering for the people every morning and every evening which consisted of a lamb, flour, oil and a portion of wine for a drink offering which was probably poured out. (Ex. 29:40) Wine was also part of other special feasts and offerings, such as firstfruits. (Lev. 23:13)

Abraham received bread and wine from Melchizedek after Abraham returned from the slaughter of the kings who had carried off Lot and his family. (Gen. 14)

As stated earlier the word "grapes" itself is not mentioned in Scripture until Genesis 40 - the account of Joseph in prison.

Dried grapes or raisins are also mentioned in Scripture. When David was hiding and wandering while waiting to become king we read of several individuals who brought him and his army of followers food, including Abigail, the wife of Nabal. (I Sam. 25:18)

In the Old Testament we discover hundreds of references to vineyards, grapes, wine and raisins. It is interesting that the use of grapes in any form was forbidden when a person took a lifetime or temporary Nazarite vow.(Num. 6:1-6) We read in the Bible of only three individuals who took a perpetual (lifetime) Nazarite vow- Samson, Samuel and John the Baptist. Otherwise grapes in various forms were a common food in Bible times.

In Numbers 13 the twelve spies were sent to search out the Promised Land. They brought back a huge cluster of grapes to show the people that God was giving them a rich and abundant life ahead, but that was not enough to encourage the Israelites to move on to that abundant life.

Therefore although they had been delivered from Egypt they were forced to wander in the wilderness for forty years. We read how the people murmured and complained. They longed for the bread, fleshpots, cucumbers, melons, leeks, onions and garlic of Egypt. I presume they also missed the grapes in their various forms because they complained to Moses:

> "And why have ye brought up the congregation of the Lord into this wilderness, that we and our cattle shall die there? And wherefore have ye made us to come up out of Egypt, to bring us to this evil place? It is no place of seed, or of figs, or of VINES, or of pomegranates..." (Num. 20:4, 5)

When the spies were sent to spy out the land of Canaan, they chose to bring back grapes, pomegranates and figs. Some of the very things the Israelites had complained they missed. Yet when they realized the Promised Land held the very things they wanted, they were afraid and allowed fear to hold them captive in the wilderness for forty years. Many had to die without enjoying all God had for them. It is tragic for us that as Christians today we yearn for the deep joy and miracle power of God but we too are afraid to move on into the promised land of this Spirit filled life. Being daily led by the Spirit seems unrealistic to us, so we ignore it or even deny it. Thank God for the "Calebs" and "Joshuas" of today who accept ALL of God's promises. Fortunately we are not forced, like these Old Testament saints, to stay with the majority and die in the wilderness. We can individually choose to develop an intimate relationship with God and know the Holy Spirit's leading and power in our lives. We can move beyond the skeptics and traditional church doctrines and enter the abundant life. We can be filled with and daily walk in the power, joy and blessings of the Holy Spirit indwelling us.

Before leaving the wilderness and entering the Promised Land Moses divided the twelve tribes of Israel into two groups. Half went to Mount Gerizim to pronounce God's blessings on the people and the other half went to Mount Ebal to pronounce the curses of God. This was to remind the people of God's covenant with them. Among the curses we find this result of disobeying God:

> "...thou shalt plant a vineyard, and shalt not gather the grapes thereof." (Deut. 28:30)

Moses reminded them that, when they were settled in the Land and enjoying all the blessings, they were to remember that it was God who had given them the land with "...vineyards and olive trees which thou plantedst not..." (Deut. 6:11) and remember it was "...the Lord thy God... that giveth thee power to get wealth..."(Deut. 8:18) Just as it was true for Israel it is true for us today. God is our true source of all wealth. It is not the government or a vocation or paycheck. Those things can disappear overnight, but God is our Jehovah- Jireh, our provider.

God gave the Israelites not only the Ten Commandments to guide their actions but also many other rules and regulations and ordinances. These were given to help them to live pure lives spiritually and physically. The rules dealt with worship, eating, washing and practical everyday living and relationships. There is an interesting law given regarding vineyards newly planted by a man who might be called into battle:

> "And what man is he that planted a vineyard, and hath not eaten of it? Let him go and return to his house, lest he die in the battle, and another man eat it." (Deut. 20:6)

During the reign of the kings of both Judah and Israel, God often reminded the Israelites that their disobedience brought curses and lack:

> "Therefore hath the curse devoured the earth and they that dwell therein are desolate... the new wine mourneth, the vine languisheth..." (Isaiah 24:6a, 7a)

> "Why then is this people of Jerusalem slidden back by a perpetual blacksliding? They hold fast deceit, they refuse to return... I will surely consume them, saith the Lord, there shall be no grapes on the vine..." (Jer. 8:5, 13a)

For Israel's idolatry, Hosea prophesies that "I (God) will destroy her vines..." (Hos. 2:12). Nahum says "The Lord hath turned away...

and marred their vine branches." (Na. 2:2). To have vineyards that produced no grapes was a terrible thing for Israel for it meant not only a valuable source of food taken from their diet but also necessary wine for drinking and to use in their ceremonial offerings.

When vineyards and grapes are mentioned in Scripture sometimes it is in the literal sense as in the references above, but sometimes symbolically. The first time we find it is used symbolically it is used prophetically. In Genesis 49, Jacob at the point of death pronounced curses and blessings upon his sons. As he speaks to Judah, Jacob prophesies this:

> "The scepter shall not depart from Judah, nor a lawgiver from beneath his feet, until Shiloh come; and unto him shall the gathering of the people be. Binding his foal unto the **vine**, and his ass's colt unto the choice **vine** he washed his garments in **wine,** and his clothes in the blood of **grapes**." (Gen. 49:10, 11)

Looking back we can see that this prophecy referred to Christ. The scepter or ruling power remained throughout the line of kings for united Israel and then Judah after the kingdom divided under Solomon's son Rehoboam. All the kings of Judah came from the lineage of David- both good and evil. God established this Messianic line in which Jesus was born. Even the governors up until the Roman Empire were of the line of David or of the Levites which were considered equal to Judah. When the Messiah, the Christ came to the earth, He brought these promised blessings. When He returns we will experience Him in His full power and blessing.

Among some Christians there is an argument about whether we need to keep the Ten Commandments today. They are Old Testament and in one sense we could say we do not need to keep them. BUT if we look at the New Testament we see Christ said just keeping the Ten Commandments was not enough- God expects more of us. All of the requirements of the Ten Commandments, except keeping the Sabbath, are found repeated in the New Testament as expectations for Christians who lived after Christ's resurrection and thus for today.

As Church Age Christians it might be easy for us to look at the Old Testament and feel it has little to teach us, but we can learn a lot about God's character and purposes. God does not change. Although it is true we no longer need to keep the Mosaic Law, there are dozens of promises that are still applicable to Christians today. Jesus told us He did not come to do away with the Law, but to complete or fulfill it.

When I took a theology course at Messiah, our college professor told us that the God of the Old Testament was more harsh and demanding, more severe and legalistic than we see Him in the New Testament Church Age. He had us read the last part of the last verse in Malachi to illustrate this: "...I come and smite the earth with a curse." He overlooked the need to read that statement in context of the chapter, which shows the true character of God- a perfect balance of holiness, love mercy, anger and judgment. God has always made it clear that He loves mankind but He also has spiritual laws for His people. Perhaps we feel God appears to be harsh in the Old Testament because we forget how much more difficult it must have been to live in those days. Man had to have outward laws because there was no provision, before Jesus came and died, for the inner man to be "quickened" or changed. The Holy Spirit could not dwell "within" the Old Testament saints but "came upon "them as they needed power to carry out God's plan. The Holy Spirit empowered individuals to do the work God had for them in order to get Israel to the Promised Land. He chose people who were listening to His voice. In the story of Gideon in the sixth chapter of the book of Judges we read this verse: "But the Spirit of the Lord **came upon** Gideon." (vs. 34) The Hebrew literally means the Spirit put on the body of Gideon to do the task. So the Old Testament people did not have a continual indwelling power, like Christians today in the Church Age, but the Spirit came upon them or took control of them to do the work God had for His people.

The Old Testament people had little or no understanding of satan and his power and influence. I was not aware of that fact until I was at a church conference where a Messianic Jew spoke. He told us how in his own life before he became a Christian, he ignorantly got involved in satanic practices. He also said that he knows of many Jewish people who get caught up in them because they have very limited understanding about the devil, yet they desire ability to get influence, power and wealth. If we look at the Old Testament without the revelation of the New Testament there is no real understanding of satan. We can only really understand who satan is when we grasp what Jesus did for mankind.

In Deuteronomy 28, we see that God made it very clear that men must make choices and those choices have automatic consequences- blessings or curses. God had to have a structured outward law in order to help people and what appears to be harshness was really mercy to help them to live productive and fulfilling lives.

Today we Christians as "engrafted Jews" (Rom. 11:17, 24) can repent from sin and be free from the curses listed in Deuteronomy 28, because Jesus took the curses upon Himself, so that we can enjoy the blessings:

> "Christ has redeemed us from the curse of the law being made a curse for us; for it is written, 'Cursed is everyone that hangeth on a tree;' that the blessing of Abraham might come on the Gentiles through Jesus Christ..." (Gal. 3:13,14a)

The way for us to be fruitful in our spiritual lives today has changed from outward laws to an inward personal relationship with God because we have the Holy Spirit in us. We can abide in the True Vine Jesus. God's purpose is the same- to make us fruitful. We should be producing grapes that are pleasing to God today just as He wanted fruit for His people Israel in the past. God symbolized this fruit as grapes to help us understand what He expects of us.

God gave us grapes as a part of a healthy diet. They are a food bursting with nutrients and vitamin C. While working on this book a neighbor of mine who lives on a large farm called to ask if I needed any concord grapes this year. Although I do have a concord grapevine there are not always enough grapes from that one vine for me to can all the juice I would like to have for the winter. The last few years I have gotten grapes from her. She and her family go up to northwestern Pennsylvania in September and bring back a truckload of juicy concord grapes to can juice for the families and for their church communion services. When I told her I wasn't sure if I needed any because I had some juice left from last year, she was quick to "enlighten" me on all the virtues of drinking grape juice everyday to build my immunity system and ward off colds and sicknesses. She is correct and it made me more regular in drinking a glass of grape juice every night before going to bed.

Recent studies have shown that grapes are cancer fighters and help to lower blood pressure. Even grape seeds have been shown to cure some diseases, such as fibromyalgia. We are reminded that God made "to grow every tree (and plant) that is pleasant to the sight and good for food". (Gen. 2:9) My family doctor told me one time that it would be good for me to drink a glass of wine every day because it was very good for lowering cholesterol. I told him I have never learned to like wine but I do can my own grape juice with the whole grape, so he said suggested I drink a glass of that every day.

In conclusion we see that Scripture includes a number of references to grapes and vineyards. In fact 31 of the 39 Old Testament books mention vineyards and/or fruit and products of grapes, such as wine and raisins. God created this fruit for man to enjoy. Grapes were a part of man's diet probably from creation. We find numerous references to vines and grapes both literally and symbolically in the Old and New Testament.

Because those living in Old Testament days could not be indwelt with God's Spirit and because the focus was on the outward and exterior laws and regulations, God used grapes to symbolize Israel and to teach spiritual lessons to them.

Today, as Christians we are grafted into the vine of Israel because in Christ we are "...Abraham's seed and heirs according to the promise." (Gal. 3:29) Although we are spiritual Jews, we are under the new covenant and the Spirit is able to indwell our "quickened" or alive spirit. The emphasis is on inner man rather than the external rules. We can also conclude that just as God made trees and vines to produce abundantly, He made humans so that they could live abundantly in all areas of life. God created us to enjoy an abundant spiritual life, as well as emotional, mental and physical life. We can learn spiritual truths from the symbolic use of grapes and vineyards as found in Scripture. There is application for us as the church today.

So we will look at two very interesting parables in the Old Testament about vines/grapes.

Think about it:

1. Wine was used as a part of the Old Testament ceremonies and worship. What is the significance of the wine?

2. Why do you think the 12 spies chose grapes, pomegranates and figs to take back to Moses and the people?

3. Would it be easier to follow clear cut outward laws than to have to interpret for ourselves what God's will is?

4. The Holy Spirit came upon people in the Old Testament to anoint them for a particular task. Today the Spirit indwells all believers. Does He still anoint or come upon us today for special tasks?

Chapter 3

Are All Branches Fruitful?

A number of years ago I sang in a choir that recorded music for a Christian radio broadcast. Besides recording songs we would give concerts at a few churches to promote the program and help raise money for the expenses of broadcasting. One evening at one of our concerts a number of people were being blessed by the words and music and raised their hands in worship. When the choir took an intermission, while they promoted the broadcast and took an offering for it, an individual from the choir told me she felt it was very wrong for people to get too emotional and raise their hands in worship. I suggested that it was okay to do that according to I Timothy 2:8 where Paul said that men should lift up holy hands to God. Her response was that it says **holy** hands and who are these people to think they were holy. I did not respond to that verbally but I took a mental and later a literal journey into Scripture. There are a number of verses that tell us we are holy. 1 Peter 2:9 and Revelation 20:6 are two of them.

I have taught the Bible for over 50 years in Sunday School, Christian boarding and day schools and at conferences. I have taught children, young people, grownups and mature Christians. I have often taught on who we are before God. From time to time I have asked the people I am teaching to stand up if they are holy. I have never had one Christian respond by standing. I understand we need to be humble and not presumptuous, but I point out to them that I am standing and they have the privilege of standing with me. They know that I am not perfect. That is not why I asked them to stand. God commands us to be holy, not perfect, and in God's eyes we are holy because He sees us through the blood of Christ. We are what God's Word tells us we are and His word calls us holy. The words "holy" and "perfect" in Scripture do not carry the idea of never making a mistake, but rather of being blameless and consecrated, committed to God. If we could not be holy or perfect spiritually, we could not enter heaven. God does not require us to be perfect or holy by what we do, but by what He did for us through Christ.

God provided a system of animal sacrifices for Israel to enable the Old Testament believers to be holy and then sent Jesus so that today we through Jesus' blood can also be holy or perfect before God. It is not a question of striving to be holy, but taking advantage of God's provision for holiness and then learning how to receive His life and power into our lives so that we produce fruit.

When I was taking a course titled <u>Major Prophets</u> at Messiah College, the parable of the vineyard in Isaiah made an impact on me. I had never noticed it before. The beautiful yet plaintive story made me stop and think about my own life as God might see it. Sometimes I found myself thinking about my spiritual life and wondering how much fruit I was producing. It was easy to be critical and judgmental looking at the Children of Israel's shortcomings and disobedience. They were God's chosen people and when I compared myself to them, I didn't feel too bad. I reasoned that I was better than they were, because I had studied their historical cycle of sin and disobedience and then repentance and then sin and idol worship again. However as I considered my own faults and failures I realized I had better not be too critical. I had failed too many times. Could God say the same parable over my life? It is a beautiful but sad illustration. Here is the parable from the Amplified Bible:

> "Let me Isaiah sing of and for my Beloved (God, the Son) a tender song of my Beloved concerning His vineyard (His chosen people). My greatly Beloved had a vineyard on a very fruitful hill. And he dug and trenched the ground and gathered out the stones from it and planted it with the choicest vine and built a tower in the midst of it. And He looked for it to bring

forth grapes, and it brought forth wild grapes. What more could have been done for my vineyard that I have not done in it? When I looked for it to bring forth grapes, why did it yield wild grapes? "(Is. 5:1-4)

Isaiah continues this parable and tells the people what God will do. The vineyard will be open to the enemy and laid waste. It was. Israel was conquered by her enemies and Jeremiah tells how the land of Judah was burned and laid waste by the Babylonian kingdom under Nebuchadnezzar. God told the people of Israel that they could not stop it and the land would be uncultivated and have no rain to bring moisture:

> "I will tell you what I will do to my vineyard; I will take away the hedge thereof, and it shall be eaten up... I will lay it waste; it shall not be pruned, nor digged, but there shall come up briers and thorns; I will also command the clouds that they rain no rain upon it." (Is. 5:5-6)

Then Isaiah makes it clear that the vineyard is Israel:

> "For the vineyard of the Lord of Hosts is the house of Israel and the men of Judah his pleasant plant." (Is. 5:7)

Whenever I read this parable I would do a self-examination. Then I would look at my church and even the churches of my community. God has done everything to make us fruitful. He has provided the Word and salvation and also the gifts and miracles needed to reach out to others. What were we doing for the people of our community and what was I doing? God has done all He can but now it is up to us. That is to say God is faithful. He does what His Word tells us He does, but we have our part to do and the Word clearly tells us what our part is. God "quickens or makes alive our spirits." He then speaks to our spirits personally through His written Word and by the Holy Spirit. The key word is "choice" It is up to me to make a choice to do what I know God is telling me or to fail to obey. There is a balance between God's work and my responsibility. The Scripture is filled with imperative verbs, i.e. words that command us to do something or tell us we have an obligation. The Word of God is filled with verbs, such as go, do, pray, study, put on, put off, love, forgive, obey and work. Paul's writings are filled with these verbs, e.g. Paul tells us in Philippians 2:12:

> "...work out (cultivate, carry out to the goal, and fully complete) your own salvation with reverence and awe and trembling(self distrust, with serious caution, tenderness of conscience, watchfulness against temptation, timidly shrinking from whatever might offend God and discredit the name of Christ." (Amp)

If you study the lives of the great men and women of God in both the Old and New Testament you will discover that they all had directions from God but they had to obey and do the work God required of them and in the manner they were told to do it. When they obeyed God all went well. Noah had to do the actual building of the ark by God's blueprints. It took work for a long time but it saved Noah and His family. He "worked out his own salvation." There are many other Biblical examples of this.

Joshua and the people of Israel took the city of Jericho by walking around it as instructed and blowing their horns at the proper time. Gideon reduced his army as God directed and fought and delivered Israel from the Midianites. Even the building of the Tabernacle was according to God's directions but the work was done by human hands. When Peter went to the home of Cornelius, God prepared him but Peter had to do the physical moving to get there. We could think of many other individuals who were told by God to do something but they had to follow His instructions and do the work.

A few times men of God tried to work out their salvation by their own method not God's and it always brought problems. Abraham listened to Sarah's plan for a son and created the Ishmaelites that are still causing problems for Israel today. King Saul fought against the Amalekites but did not destroy all that God told him to destroy. God rejected Saul as king over Israel after his disobedience. His descendants lost the succession to the throne of Israel. Even Moses disobeyed God's instructions and struck the rock instead of speaking to it and never personally reached the Promised Land.

These examples remind us that we have a responsibility and a choice to obey God gives us work to do and it must be done in God's way to be a spiritual success and victory. Even when God showed me the house I was to buy, I had to wait for God's timing and when the time came I had to take action to purchase it.

Sometimes direction comes from God not just for physical action but for a mental or emotional attitude change. We need to adjust our thoughts and attitudes, in order to develop spiritual maturity. We must not ignore God when He directs us regarding our time and money and prayer, as well as developing more love and forgiveness. When we obey God's leading we will develop and grow spiritually

Paul in Colossians tells us that we need to "put off" and to "put on" certain actions and attitudes. We make the choice. We work out our salvation. Two things we fail to see in many churches found in Colossians 3:13, 14 are love (charity) and forgiveness. We Christians tend to be less loving and forgiving toward our brothers and sisters in the church than toward the world.

One very basic command of God is "love." Love is a necessity for us as Christians. In fact God's Word tells us that rules and traditions do not "count for anything, but only faith activated and energized and expressed and working THROUGH LOVE" (Gal. 5:6 Amp). Love for others and for God brings growth and enables us to obey the rest of the instructions in Colossians 3:8-14. It will cause good fruit to be produced in our lives. The kind of fruit I produce will be the result of the kind of life I live. I cannot control the fruit but I can control the attitudes and actions that make the fruit. The fruit of my life will show what I really am inside. The kind of fruit does not determine the type of vine, but the type of vine to which we are connected produces the kind of fruit. When I see the fruit it tells me what the vine is and so it is in our lives. What I am within will eventually show up in the fruit seen on the outside.

As I realized the significance of that truth I began to meditate on another parable about fruit that had often puzzled me. One that I felt I didn't completely understand - The Sower and the Seed. It is recorded in three of the four Gospels and I had heard a good many sermons from it but what I had never heard explained was "...and bring forth fruit, some thirty-fold, some sixty, and some an hundred" (Mk. 4:20) I didn't understand why some people produced more fruit that others. Was it based on God or works? Did God foreordain or predetermine the amount? The balance between God's part and my part became clearer. One night I had a dream. I was in a jewelry store and wanted to buy a ring. Now I do not like rings, but in the dream I was going to get one. I was shown rings with a wide variety of value from ten dollars up to thousands. As I was trying to decide which ring I wanted, I realized the value of the ring I chose was up to me. It was my decision. After I awoke and asked God the meaning of that dream He revealed to me that it was like my life. I must choose how valuable my life will be by choosing how much fruit I wanted to bring forth and that will depend on my relationship to the Vine- Jesus. What was I willing to do or how much time and effort was I willing to put into my relationship with God knowing He was the source of abundant fruit. Was I willing to abide and live in Him to get the one hundredfold? The amount and quality of fruit produced was my choice. God gave me the gifts and power and direction He knew I would need to serve Him and He would produce fruit though me to the degree of my surrender to Him and my obedience to His Word and to the Holy Spirit.

Recently I bought and read a very challenging book by a woman by the name of Lori Wilke. She has a ministry called Spirit to Spirit Ministry. The book is entitled **The Costly Anointing**. It is a tremendous teaching on the way to gain a fruitful life but as the title suggests it costs us something. She discusses this concept of the thirty, sixty and hundredfold life. It is published by Destiny Image and I would recommend reading it if one desires to live a more fruitful abundant life.

As Christians we need to find and keep a balance between God's part and our responsibility. It is easy for us as humans to move in extremes either one way or the other. I can sit back and say God must do all the changing in me. If He wants me to do something He will make me do it. On the other hand I can be so eager to serve God I run off in all directions doing everything on my own ability and strength. Either of these two extremes will bring defeat. It is important that we learn the Scriptural balance of what God does in, for, and through us and what we are responsible to do.

As I spent time meditating on God's Word about fruit, vines and vineyards, the Lord began to show me more spiritual truths in the parables about vines. This study led me to the parable of the Wicked Husbandmen. This too had always been a parable I did not completely comprehend. As I studied and meditated on the story, the Lord showed me that the Jews in Jesus' day knew exactly what He was saying to them. I could know, too, so I waited upon Him to bring me a "rhema" word, i.e. personal revelation knowledge from this parable. I began to see some common principles in the different parables in the Bible. God spoke truth in the Old Testament parables to teach His people just as He taught spiritual truths through Jesus' parables. There was more to a parable than a simple story.

God gave Isaiah a beautiful, though sad, parable about a vineyard that failed to produce fruit, because He wanted more than His people were producing. God has always provided and still provides all we need to have the abundant life, but just as Israel fell short of the promises we can do the same today.

It is sad that we today many times fail to read and study the Old Testament and therefore miss some basic truths in understanding what God says in the New Testament.

Isaiah's parable is the basis for the whole study and purpose of this book. It will help us to understand how to experience the abundant life Jesus promised and enable us to look at our lives and see what kind of fruit we are producing. Then learn how to produce good fruit to attract others to the Christian life.

There are lessons to learn from the parables of vines and fruit. They are important because we need to find the balance in our lives related to what God does and what we need to do to produce fruit. My desire is to produce the one hundred fold and to produce palatable fruit for others to see Christ in me. We do not want to produce bad fruit or limited fruit that keeps me a spiritual baby and hinders others from wanting to follow Jesus. A proper understanding of Isaiah's parable challenges us and also opens our understanding of the Vineyard Parable told by Jesus.

When we understand that the Jewish leaders in Jesus' day knew this parable given by Isaiah and understood God was chiding their forefathers because they had produced no fruit for God, we will see how they interpreted and understood Jesus' parable of the Wicked Husbandmen in His vineyard parable. We can also understand the illustration given by Jesus in John 15 concerning the Vine and branches.

Think about it:

1. How do you work out your salvation in your daily Christian walk? How can you keep a balance between works and faith?

2. What would our world be like today if Abraham had not run ahead of God?

3. Have you ever run ahead of God? What were the results? How can I stay in God's timing for my life?

Chapter 4

A Fruitless Vine - Jotham's Story

When I was growing up my grandparents lived with us and so I had the benefit (?) of four adults enlightening me with wise sayings, fables, illustrations, and stories filled with morals and secrets for proper and happy living. Among them were the stories, familiar to many, about the boy who cried wolf and the race between the tortoise and the hare. There were also sermons in a sentence like the saying that "a stitch in time saves nine." and "those who live in glass houses shouldn't throw stones." There are many common ones that were spoken to me and have been passed down for ages. Some of these were easy to understand. Others I must admit seemed to have little application to my life at the time, but became real to me later in life when I was in the middle of a problem - usually self-made. If I had remembered the saying about "saving up for a rainy day" I might have been a better manager of my money.

When I finished college and started teaching it was wonderful to have a paycheck every two weeks. When I got it, I felt it was mine and I could spend it any way I pleased and I found many things that pleased me. I would spend my full paycheck long before the next one came and as the saying goes I had too much month left at the end of my money. It seemed when the various bills came in at the end of the month my paycheck was mostly gone and I had to struggle to pay the necessary bills. I had no plan for saving for an emergency and never worried about a "rainy day."

Then an unexpected emergency came and I had to find someone from whom I could borrow what I needed. I was embarrassed and hated to do it and thought about the saving for a rainy day maxim. After several difficult experiences I learned to put money into savings each month and how to use my money more wisely. Sometimes we learn the hard way, but I am thankful I did learn the meaning of saving for a rainy day.

The story about the boy who cried wolf I understood earlier in life. As a child I had a vivid imagination and could make up all kinds of stories. However after a while I learned that people didn't believe anything I told them even when it was true, because I had told so may made-up tales. I learned to make sure my listeners knew what was a true story and what I was making up.

Teaching by story and illustrations has existed for centuries. The Jewish people were familiar with this method of learning. God used stories, symbolic actions and parables to help His children understand spiritual truths. Jesus was a master at storytelling. We call His stories parables – earthly stories with a heavenly meaning. We find them recorded in God's Word.

The interesting thing about parables is that they can be understood on various levels and teach several truths. As we allow the Holy Spirit to speak to us we can get more and deeper revelation from the parables, but we need to remember not to take them too far in detail because they are still only stories. They must always teach us truths and principles which are supported by other Scriptures.

Although teaching in parables is usually connected with Jesus (there are over 30 recorded for us in the four Gospels) teaching in parables is not unique or limited to Jesus' ministry. It is a fact that we can read more parables told by Jesus than any other Biblical character, but there are over a half dozen interesting parables in the Old Testament. The books of the major and minor prophets, as well as the historical books, include parables. In fact God tells us through Hosea that He sent prophets to act out parables "I have spoken to you by the prophets...and have appealed to you through parables acted out by the prophets." (Hos. 12:10 Amp.) Two Old Testament parables make reference to vines. By looking at these parables it gives us better understanding of the one Jesus told about the wicked husbandmen. The Jews to whom He was speaking would have been well acquainted with the Old Testament. It is important that we are aware of what the Jews would understand about the symbolic use of grapevines in the Scriptures when Jesus told the parable of the Wicked Husbandmen. They knew exactly what Jesus was trying to tell them. So we will look at two Old Testament parables known by the Jewish people who listened to Jesus' teaching. The first one we will look at is in Judges 9.

The historical age covered in the book of Judges is difficult to date, but it covers the period of time from Joshua's death to the choosing of the first king, Saul. It was a time of spiritual and ethical upheaval when "every man did that which was right in his own eyes" (Jud. 17:6)

As different individuals were called by God they would judge and lead Israel. They were called to be military deliverers. One of the better known judges named Gideon had a son by the name of Abimelech, born of a concubine. After the death of Gideon, Abimelech decided that he should lead Israel in his father's place, but Gideon had seventy-one other sons. Abimelech managed to kill them all except the youngest named Jotham who hid himself. Then Abimelech declared himself king. At this point Jotham went up to Mount Gerizim and spoke the parable recorded in Judges 9. An understanding of the parable symbols will be a help in understanding this parable and the vineyard parables.

In His parable Jotham told how the trees wanted to anoint a king over them. They first went to the olive tree, then the fig tree and then the vine, but none of them wanted to be king. Finally the trees decided that they would go to the bramble and ask the bramble to be king. The bramble was delighted to take on this position of power. The intent of the story was to show Abimelech that the men he had gathered around him had not asked a useful or worthy leader but a bramble. The first three plants were interested in producing something good for mankind and did not want to be king, but the useless proud bramble liked power and glory. That was the meaning of the parable to Abimelech and his men. However, the parable which was given to Jotham came from God and it has futuristic implications, as well as fitting the situation of Israel at that moment. The people of Israel were seeking their identity in the world around them rather than in God. They wanted a political heritage as well as a spiritual one. Perhaps even more.

In Scripture the olive tree represents their spiritual heritage, but their disobedience had turned their relationship to God into a meaningless ritualistic performance. The fig tree, which is their national identity had been lost because they had failed to conquer their enemies and allow God to be their king and military strategist. To understand the vine we need to consider John 15. Jesus is the Vine. This parable foretells that Jesus will also be rejected by the Jews and He will not be made King of their lives. Furthermore in end times Israel will find the bramble and will follow him. This will be the anti-Christ who will appear and convince the Jews that he can be trusted to rebuild the temple and be a worthy world leader to establish peace on earth.

The Jews trusted their heritage not the God of their heritage. They said to Jesus "We be Abraham's seed." (Jn. 8:33) They took great pride spiritually in being Jews. Jesus was speaking to them about knowing the truth and being free. They were in bondage and did not even realize it. They not only rejected their Messiah but found security in their traditions and bondage. They felt no need of something new and better from God. Jesus was offering a new covenant but they were content with the old.

This is not the first time we see the vine used symbolically of Israel. Jesus was THE Vine whom God foreordained to redeem, not only Israel from her sins, but the whole world. He would come from the vineyard of the nation Israel.

If we would compare ourselves with the Children of Israel we might be quick to say we are not like they were. We know who Jesus is. Yet we can be in the church and be bound by traditions and have no freedom in Christ. We think we are fine, but in actuality our traditions and programs are the main focus rather than Christ. We cannot worship without being in our comfort zone of "we always do it this way." We think because our parents and grandparents always went to church, had membership in the Christian church and always practiced certain forms of worship and ordinances that we need to follow the same patterns and everything will be right. We do not differentiate between traditions and Biblical concepts. I have a friend who calls it the "Second Generation" syndrome. It can attack Christians of the second, third or even the tenth generation. We must keep a first generation newness in our relationship with Christ or it will become only an event and practice.

I did not have the privilege of being raised in a Christian home. My parents were good people and had high standards of morality, but I didn't go to church until I was in fifth grade and didn't really commit my life to Christ until I was 14. Since that time I have attended a number of different churches and I have seen people who take great pride in their heritage. They attend church faithfully. They have their list of "do's" and "don't's". When I first became a Christian I adopted the list from those brought up in the church. My mind was being trained to show that I was a Christian by the way I dressed and the type of entertainment I chose, or rather didn't choose. What I needed was an intimate relationship with Christ, but it took me a number of years before I understood and experienced that. Christians are right in wanting a pure life but we sometimes don't know how to get it. We put forth our best effort to become pure before God by our works, but that is backwards. When I was teaching in a Christian school, I had one of my students bring in a book from their church that actually stated if you get yourself correct looking and acting on the outside that the inside will take care of itself. They sincerely believed that somehow righteousness and holiness would work its way into the individual's heart if they got the outside looking and behaving properly.

I believe we can be saved but never mature in Christ because we are bound by traditions and self righteousness and don't know it. Others follow traditions and practices and have never personally accepted Christ into their hearts. Being born into a Christian home has its advantages. Having a Christian heritage can be a blessing, but it can also be dangerous because some people count on their heritage to save them and to bring liberty, joy and eternal life. It won't. It too often brings the "Second Generation" complex. Not relationship but religion. This existed in the church where I got saved and still exists in many churches.

A pastor I know used an illustration that compares our life to being like one of three chairs. If we are sitting in the first chair we are sitting in the unsaved place of sinfulness. The second chair according to his idea is the chair of doing and doing. This is the person who is very busy doing good things. That is not a bad place to be in some ways but it can make a person tired. It is the Christian who is busy doing things to stay under God's favor. It is often based on the belief that we can get to heaven and get our prayers answered because of **our** good works. This is the chair many second generation Christians occupy. The third chair is one of rest because it is a chair of relationship and intimacy with God. We are still doing good for God but are doing it with His direction and empowerment- not works for works sake but in obedience to what God wants for our particular life and giftings. However I think there is a fourth chair. I think there is one between that pastor's first and second chair and I call it a highchair. It is where the baby Christians sit and stay because they never grow up or mature. Some second generation Christians sit there because they think they come from a long line of Christians so everything is fine with them and God.

"Second generation" Christians can concentrate so much on outward issues that are traditions and "the way we always do it" that they miss the joy of a real relationship with God.

I remember after I was first saved most Bible facts and knowledge were new and exciting to me. I was eager to hear all I could in church. Although the young people my age all sat near the back of the church during services and were busy whispering and writing notes to each other, I wanted to sit up front so I wouldn't miss anything. I learned years later that some of the teens were unhappy about my sitting up front and listening because their parents wanted them to do the same and compared them to me. That was not the best way to make friends.

Also as I started attending youth meetings I was amazed when we would have Bible quiz games and competitions that those teens knew so many facts from Scripture. I think they were as amazed at me because I knew so little about the Bible.

One time the youth were planning a talent night. My sister and I use to often sing together so we were encouraged to participate in the program. We did not know many Christian hymns or songs since we were still new to church and we sang the only hymn we knew. After we sang the hymn "Abide with Me" I was embarrassed to be informed by one of the teens that that hymn is only to be sung at funerals and it was weird to sing it at a youth meeting. I know our hearts were right in wanting to sing a hymn but we lacked the "traditions" connected with a hymn. It is all too easy for "second generation" Christians to make new Christians feel spiritually inferior and confused between Biblical truth and traditions.

This is not unlike the Jews in Jesus' day. They had the "second generation" complex, but passed down from MANY previous generations. It was based mostly on behavior and actions rather than a meaningful and vital relationship with God. They KNEW all the right things to do to keep the law, but had lost their communion with the Jehovah God of Abraham and Moses. They kept reminding themselves and others that they were of the root of Abraham. Jesus confronted this attitude via parables such as the Wicked Husbandmen.

It is like Christians today who almost always talk about the "good old days" of revival and encounters with God. Yet tell nothing about what God said or did today.

Scripture has a number of parables which teach spiritual truth by way of vines and vineyards. We have looked at Jotham's parable about the Vine to give us a better understanding and background to discover truth in other parables. This will enable us to mature and exemplify Christ by our fruitfulness. The abundant life does not consist of knowing all the church traditions and rules. It is not simply the way we look on the outside, although it may affect our appearance. It is our relationship with God.

The simple parable recorded in Judges was an illustration given to the Israelites to help them see they were making a poor choice in whom they were going to follow as their leader. Abimelech was a worthless and evil deceiver but the men of Shechem ignored the story and chose him to judge them. In time they turned against him and more violence erupted. The details of the story can be found in Judges 10.

We as Christians today need to know who we are to follow. We need to set priorities in life as to the true source of direction to go in order to bear valuable fruit. Church traditions and men's ideas are not necessarily wrong but the Word of God is the final authority and above church traditions. I heard a Jewish rabbi once say that if there was a dispute between Jewish tradition and what Scripture said the rabbi's word was of greater authority. Does the Christian church take that stand?

This chapter has discussed two important issues about the parable related by Jotham. We need to see it is a basis for understanding the parable Jesus told of the Wicked Husbandmen. The Jews understood what Jesus was saying when he related the parable of the Wicked Husbandmen. but maybe even more importantly it helps us take a look at our own lives and check to see if we have a "second generation" Christian concept and are caught up more with traditions and doing than in developing an intimate relationship with God.

As we continue to study more about the symbolical use of vines and fruit from Scripture we hopefully will see that being a Christian is not just doing but being. It will make us fruitful and allow us to enjoy the abundant life Jesus promised to His children. It will give us a basis for understanding the kinds of grapes or fruit produced in followers of Christ.

Today some Christians who have a Christian heritage are typically "second generation" Christians. They might be as fruitless and spiritually lacking as the Jews during Jesus' ministry on earth. Christianity is not just a routine way of life passed down from generation to generation. It is not a habit or a heritage. We can learn how to live the abundant life. It is a vibrant life!

Think about it

1. What are the advantages of teaching in stories or parables?

2. How are second generation Christians like the Jews in the Old testament?

3. What are the characteristics of second generation Christians? Do you know any? How can you help them to make changes in their lives?

4. Do you think that Jotham had any understanding of the futuristic implications of his parable? Why or why not?

Chapter 5

A Fruitless Vineyard according to Jesus

As I said before, I was not brought up in a Christian home, but as a very small child I was taken to a nearby church for Sunday School. My parents did not go to church but thought it was a good idea for us to be educated in the Bible. For a year or so my father dropped off my two older sisters and me on Sunday mornings at a major denominational church a few miles away. My father said he had little use for the church because some of the members that he knew went to the local tavern and caroused on Saturday nights and then went to church on Sunday. He would stay home Saturday and Sunday.

I do not know how long we were taken to that church but we only went to Sunday School and it was only for a short time because his job required him to work on Sundays for a while and we didn't go to Sunday School. By the time he was back to his schedule of being off Sundays we no longer went. I don't remember learning anything from the Bible during that time but I was very young. About the only thing I remember was that at the end of class all the children gathered together in a circle in a center main room, and I didn't want to join them. I was very bashful and although my teacher tried to get me to join I stubbornly refused. I didn't really like going. I am not sure how old I was, but I know it was before I started school at age five. There was no such thing as kindergarten in those days so I went to first grade in a one room schoolhouse where the teacher taught first grade through eighth grade in one room. I do remember a lot more about my school days. I know we started each morning with Bible reading. Sad to say

I don't remember anything from those times as far as learning Bible stories or lessons.

The first Bible story I remember hearing was actually in public school when a Christian lady would come every so often and teach Bible stories to all of us. I was fascinated with the wonders of flannel graph depicting characters and events from the Bible. She had beautiful backgrounds of rooms and scenery that at times did not seem to change quite fast enough for me.

The first story I remember hearing was about Noah and the rainbow. I had often seen rainbows in the sky but had never heard what they represented or where they came from. The whole idea of the world being flooded and the promise that it wouldn't ever happen again seemed unreal to me. I had no idea what was in the Bible but I had never heard that story before. I needed to read it for myself. I knew we had a Bible at home on one of the bookshelves in our living room but it was something with which we children didn't play. One day when no one was around I found it and looked for the story about Noah and the rainbow.

As you might guess I couldn't find it. I was completely illiterate when it came to Scripture. I didn't know what Old and New Testament meant or what the names of the various books were. I just knew I couldn't find any story about Noah. I began to wonder if it was just a fairy tale like the story of Cinderella or Snow White. One of my favorite books that I read and reread many times was a collection of Grimm's fairy tales. I felt a sort of disappointment because the teacher of the Bible stories said they were true not like the fairy tales I had read and knew were made up tales. When I heard these Bible stories, they seemed different to me and I wanted to believe that the stories we heard were true, but I couldn't find anything about Noah in the pictureless small print Bible with its hundreds of pages. In time I accepted the stories as true because of the way the teacher explained them, even though I myself was unable to find them. I did not understand it then, but I later realized there is a power in the Word of God that made me believe.

When I got to fifth grade a schoolmate invited my sister and me to go to Sunday School with her and through the kindness of the church deacon I began attending a church where the people helped me learn a great deal about the Bible and what it meant to be a Christian.

By the time I graduated from high school I had accepted Christ as my Savior and chose to attend Messiah College where I had a number of Bible courses. One course was on the teachings of Christ from which I learned a lot and which made me want to have a deeper understanding of all the parables taught by Jesus.

The parables always interested me but there were a few I didn't really understand even after this course and one of these was the parable of the Wicked Husbandmen. I didn't understand why the husbandmen didn't give a few grapes and say that's all there were. Only in the last few years did the Lord show me the meaning of it

I had always looked at it from my understanding and point of view. God directed me to look at the parable of the Wicked Husbandmen as the Jews hearing it from Jesus must have understood it.

As Jesus rode into the city of Jerusalem to celebrate His last Passover Feast with His disciples, the crowd shouted praises to Him. By this time, however, the religious leaders were deeply disturbed with Jesus and His teachings. The opposition toward Him was escalating rapidly. The Jewish crowd shouted "Hosanna to the Son of David." The people who had gathered for the feast saw Jesus as the Messiah who would deliver them. However most of them saw Him as a political liberator. They called Him "the King that cometh in the name of the Lord." The Pharisees instructed Jesus to rebuke these people. They felt they must put an end to Jesus' influence with the people.

Jesus was well aware of the growing opposition and even as he heard the public acclamation, He had to know what was ahead for Him. The people would quickly reverse their praise into cries of "crucify Him!"

On the last Tuesday and Wednesday before His crucifixion, the chief priests and scribes blatantly challenged Jesus' authority. During this time the religious leaders hoped to trap Jesus. During this period of controversy Jesus told a number of parables. One of these was the "Wicked Husbandmen" Perhaps He was giving the religious leaders one last chance to accept Him as the awaited Messiah, but they continued to see Him only as a threat to their power and control over the religious life of the Jews.

In this parable Jesus was telling the Jews that He was the Son of God and He was going to be killed. I understood that part. Jesus was reminding them that as the vineyard Israel they had always killed the prophets and now they were going to kill the very Son of God. All of that was obvious to me. Then one day as I was reading this story the Lord revealed that there was more to the parable. This parable held a very serious accusation against the Jewish leaders and I was seeing only the surface of the parable. The Jewish leaders were trying to kill Jesus just as their forefathers had often killed the prophets God had sent. They **knew** Jesus was the Messiah but **chose** to reject Him. They knew Old Testament prophecy. In the Gospel of John, John tells us that "the world was made by Him, and the **world knew** Him **not**." but the next verse tells us that "He came unto His own and His **own received** Him **not**" Their rejection of Jesus was a deliberate act. They wanted their own selfish control, power and authority over Israel. They did not want to submit to God's authority. Like the husbandmen in the parable who knew it was not their vineyard they thought by killing the son the vineyard would belong to them. They wanted to interpret the Law for their advantage and wanted to keep their positions. They knew Jesus was a threat to their authority and wanted to do away with Him.

They also would have been familiar with the parable in Isaiah 5 and I believe they also knew Jesus was telling them that there were no grapes in the vineyard. They might be controlling the vineyard but it had no profitable fruit unto God.

It was at this time of trying to think this through that I heard a Messianic Jew talking about the Torah and Old Testament Scriptures versus the written rabbinical law. As I stated in an earlier chapter He made the statement that if a question arises among the Jews the FINAL authority is the rabbinical law not Scripture. That would probably have been the practice when Jesus came to redeem Israel.

Just as God chose the priests and leaders to be His representatives to care for the vineyard of Israel, so the owner in the parable had the husbandmen doing the work in his vineyard. The religious leaders like the husbandmen wanted the vineyard (Israel) under their authority.

They wanted to "own" the Jewish people and be in full control. But God owned the vineyard and was over Israel. The Jewish people belonged to Him not to the religious leaders who felt they were the ones in charge of the nation. These religious leaders loved their religious system and traditions more than they loved the promises of God and the prophecy of a coming Messiah. They couldn't even recognize or deliberately chose to not recognize Jesus as the Messiah, because He didn't fit their preconceived and traditional ideas of God.

In the church today we can see a similar attitude. Some of us are so set in our traditions and preconceived ways of thinking that we do not even allow the Scripture to speak to us. Instead of reading the Word to learn truth we read it to support what we already believe. We do not want change and therefore miss the "new every morning" aspect of God and become fruitless in our lives and send people away. In fact we scare away the people who are looking for a fulfilling life because they don't see joy and excitement in us, but rather rules and formalism.

In the study of this and the other symbolic uses of vines and fruit God began teaching me the whole concept of the symbolism of vines and grapes. God showed me what was really being said by Jesus. There were no edible grapes or no grapes at all. The husbandmen had nothing to give the owner of the vineyard just as the Jewish religious leaders had no fruit to offer God from their teaching and leading. I was eager to begin to look up other Scriptures that talked about grapes and vineyards. I could only remember the one from Isaiah, but discovered a number of other places in Scripture that used vines and grapes symbolically.

We know that as Jesus told this parable of the wicked vineyard keepers that the Jewish leaders listening would have been very familiar with the whole symbolism of vineyards and grapes. They would think about the fact that the husbandmen had no grapes or only had wild grapes to give, because they were familiar with Isaiah 5.

When I went back to Isaiah 5, I realized I had forgotten the facts of the story. I had always remembered it as a vine that produced no grapes but it says it produced only "wild grapes." I began to wonder what wild grapes were and if there was more symbolism using grapes to be found in other places

It was this revelation that led to my searching the Scriptures to discover different types of worthless grapes mentioned. I discovered references not only to no grapes or wild grapes, but also bitter and sour grapes. I began to wonder what the significance of the different types of grapes- none, wild, bitter and sour- could be for Christians today. It challenged me to let God show me what kind of grapes the church was producing today then to examine my own life to see what my fruit was. It was time to learn what God wanted to teach us in His use of different kinds of grapes.

If we want to learn from the symbolism of vineyards and grapes it is important for us to understand both the parables of Isaiah's teaching and Jesus' teaching. This is the secret to understanding the other references to different types of grapes produced by God's children. We need to also keep in mind when looking at the whole symbolism of vines and fruit that Jesus taught about Himself as the True Vine. We are familiar with this teaching but the Jewish leaders probably did not hear that illustration because the concept of Jesus being the True Vine was given privately to the 12 disciples on the last Thursday evening before Jesus died on the cross.

Think about it

1. Do people today know that Jesus is the Son of God but choose to reject Him? Why?

2. How does knowing John 15 help us today in understanding better the symbolic use of vines and fruitful branches?

3. Are there Christians in churches today who want to control the church's programs and people in it? What can we do about it?

4. Can a church be so steeped in tradition and styles of worship that they actually turn the unsaved away from God?

Chapter 6

Grapes Can Be Wild

When I was growing up in the fifties, like many other teenagers, I spent many hours listening to the popular singers and singing groups of the day. I was enchanted with the Platters singing about "Twilight Time", and the Everly Brothers telling me "All I have to do is Dream", and the wonderful sounds of Connie Francis, Perry Como, Pat Boone and many others. I listened to a very powerful Buffalo radio station whose call letters were WKBW. I could hear it not only in the rural farm region where I lived but up to over 300 miles away. I was very surprised when one day someone told me that this powerful radio station had in years past been owned by a large church in Buffalo. The letters WKBW actually stood for Well Known Bible Witness. The church crumbled after the pastor ran off with the church secretary and the church money. It had been a real scandal and the fall of a great ministry. Although I do not know the details of how this came about I am sure it was not a thought that came suddenly out of nowhere. James instructs us:

> "But every person is tempted when he is drawn away, enticed, and baited by his own evil desire(lust, passions). Then the evil desire, when it has conceived, gives birth to sin..." (Jas. 1:14, 15 Amp.)

Overt sin starts as a little secret (not to God) thought and if not dealt with eventually it becomes a hidden action and then often public

38

knowledge and disgrace. We use the term "hidden sin" but there really is no such thing to God.

Although the fall of this ministry was a tragic event, we know it is an all too common one, especially in the last couple decades. We do not know the pressure from demonic forces that the leaders of ministries face today, but we have all experienced our own personal temptations so we are not to stand in judgment of others. Scripture warns us:

> "Who art thou that judgest another man's servant? To his own master he standeth of falleth." (Rom. 4:14)

God instructs us what to do when we see a brother (or sister) sin, but condemning or judging them is not part of the instructions. The word for judge as used here means to avenge, sentence or damn. This does not mean we ignore the sin but we are told to "restore such an one in the spirit of meekness, considering <u>thyself</u>, lest thou also be tempted." (Gal. 6:1) One of our biggest reactions to a situation of this sort should be to examine ourselves to be cleansed of any of our own known or secret sins.

Secret sins always bring bad fruit, even when they do not become a story on the news media. They hinder us by limiting our spiritual power and influence and even in receiving answers to our prayers. I believe Scripture refers to secret sin(s) as wild grapes.

The term wild grapes is used only two times in the King James Bible. Both references are in Isaiah 5. This is the parable given by God to Isaiah about Israel. God explains how He had planted a vineyard and cared for it properly and lovingly. He did everything that was necessary to produce an abundant crop, but it produced "wild grapes." According to Strong's Concordance, the Hebrew word used for wild grapes is a poison berry- a berry that gives off a stench.

God chose Abraham to establish a righteous line for a double purpose- not only to create a lineage in which the Messiah and Redeemer could come into the world, but also for Israel to be a model nation whose actions would be an example of Who God was to the surrounding nations. God never was exclusive. He is redemptive in nature, but He is holy and He chose Abraham because Abraham believed in God and heard Him speak. The way to God was open to the non-Jewish if they would accept Him and obey His laws. Is it possible that if Israel had continued to serve God and not repeatedly sinned that they would have produced "sweet fruit" that would cause others to be drawn to Jehovah God? We cannot know because God's people turned to evil and worshiped idols, thus producing "wild grapes."

God's people need to produce sweet grapes that will bring others to Him but at times we produce wild grapes and that causes people to turn away from God.

There are some Christian ministries that know that as the government makes more laws about equal opportunity in employment (including hiring homosexuals) they may someday be forced to hire people who are not Christians and this could be harmful to their witness. That is understandable, but if that day comes can we be so much like Jesus and so pure before God and so filled with love and the Holy Spirit and so consistently living for Jesus that these people will either want what we have or want to get as far away from us as possible? Do we today live in such a way that we need to separate ourselves from the world for fear we will be influenced to become like them? Perhaps today so many Christians are so much like the world that there is no noticeable difference.

That is what was happening to the Israelites. They did not bring redemption to the heathen but let the heathen lead them into sin. We must not be too hard on the Israelites for they did not have the knowledge or power of the New Testament saints. The Holy Spirit did not indwell them. Therefore whole nations of people who were controlled and even in some cases possessed by demons had to be destroyed because they worked against Israel and if they dwelt among Israel, they led Israel into idol worship, instead of Israel leading these nations to God. The real battle was a spiritual one between God and satan. The Jews were meant to show the world that Jehovah was the One True God who had created the earth and all the people and nations on it. It was possible for any person to accept the God of Abraham and become a part of the people of God. God made provision through the laws for that. These individuals were known as proselytes. God had a heart for the world and I think He meant Israel to be the first missionaries to the heathen, but because they would get caught up in idol worship so quickly, God did what He had to do to keep them pure and holy before Him, in order to produce a line of people who were spiritually obedient enough to produce an earthly father and mother of faith to be capable of raising His Son.

There are several Biblical accounts of Gentiles accepting the Jehovah God of Israel. One of these was Rahab and her family who were spared when the rest of Jericho fell (Jos. 6). Another was Ruth the Moabitess. The people of Moab descended from incest between Lot and his daughter (Gen. 19). They hated the Jews and refused to let Israel pass through their land on Israel's journey to Canaan. Later in history we read they sent for Balaam to curse Israel (Nu. 22-24). Yet we discover when Ruth left her people and chose to follow the God of her mother-in-law, she was accepted into Israel. Ruth, as well as Rahab, became a part of the lineage of Christ and are the only two women mentioned in Jesus' earthly father's ancestry. (Mat. 1) God wanted to save all mankind - the Jew first and then the Gentile. The Jews could have been "missionaries "to the heathen, but instead they copied the Gentile world. Then when the Jews rejected their Messiah, God sent Paul to the Gentiles. Jesus came to the Jews first.

God chose Abraham and guided him through the birth of Isaac and dealt with Jacob to raise up a people called Israel. He kept His hand upon them through feast and famine. He delivered them from Egypt and brought them into the Promised Land with countless miracles. He helped them overcome the enemies and establish a country. He had worked with them through their stubborn insistence for a king and through the division of the twelve tribes into Israel and Judah. The majority of kings only led the people into sin and idolatry. After Israel became a divided nation under King Rehoboam the Northern Kingdom did not have one righteous king and God let them be taken into captivity by Assyria in 732 BC. The southern kingdom of Judah lasted a bit longer because they had eight kings who attempted to lead the people back to God. Some succeeded better than others, but Judah continued to move away from God. God sent the prophet Isaiah to Judah to warn them to repent or they too would be taken captive. This was the setting for this beautiful, but melancholy parable. As

God viewed his vineyard and the vine that was to produce "The True Vine" (Jn. 15) all God could see was wild grapes. This parable reveals the grief of God for His people.

As I stated earlier I thought it said no grapes and I stopped to consider if I had any fruit for God in my life. When I reread it and discovered it talked about wild grapes, I looked at myself a little differently. I asked God if He saw wild grapes being produced in my life and in His church and children of today. Are we corporately or individually producing wild grapes? What did wild grapes look like? What were wild grapes?

What do the unsaved see as they look at the Christians in their beautiful buildings today? Are we a poison berry to them? Do we actually give out a stench that drives them away or keeps them from getting too close to us? What things are in the church that might be symbolic of a wild grape?

I asked God to show me what wild bad smelling grapes we might be producing in the church today. A verse came to my mind: "Dead flies cause the ointment of the apothecary to send forth a stinking smell, so doth a little folly him that is in reputation for wisdom and honour." (Ec. 10:1). The word "folly" carries the idea of lacking good sense.

When I was growing up people looked at the church and Christians as honorable and trustworthy people. Christians were shown respect. In our society today it seems like it is just the opposite. It would be easy to dismiss that shift of opinion by blaming the world for becoming more openly sinful and hateful. I am sure that is part of the reason for the change, but I am not convinced it is the only reason. Have Christians become more like the world? Have we allowed society to dictate selfish actions and attitudes upon us? Sin seems to be as common among church people as the world. The divorce rate and broken homes among Christians is about equal to the world's. We have become more self-centered. satan has sent a deceptive "spirit of entitlement" to cause people today, especially Americans, to feel we have rights rather than privileges. We see it on the highways and in the workplaces. All this has affected the church and even some influential public ministries making it easier for satan to turn unsaved people away from the church. They figure we have no answers for their needs because we aren't living and doing any better than they are. This spirit can affect Christians, but it will eventually produce wild grapes.

Sometimes we Christians are guilty of hiding sins and sinful practices. God in His grace and mercy will continue to speak to us but allow us to go on choosing to disobey. Interestingly enough He can even use us for a while to serve in ministries and win the unsaved, but eventually our sin will be revealed. Then what happens to the ones we had influenced for good? We cause offense to them.

While I was in missionary service in Africa a number of years ago, I attended a church conference. In the evening we had one of our church leaders preaching and he did give an effective evangelistic message and many people repented or rededicated their lives to Christ. But in his life he was holding secret sin. He was actually living a double life. He had two different wives and families in two different places. This was not discovered until a few months later. How was that possible? God still used him in his calling. Romans 11:29 tells us that "...the gifts and calling of God are without repentance." The Amplified Bible uses the word irrevocable. God will allow us to use the gifts He has given us, but hidden sin will finally come out. This man repented like others in ministry have, but most ministries are weakened and remain weak even after the individual(s) have repented.

We cannot hold on to secret sins and reach the full potential of God's calling on our life. Our secret sins are known by God, and although we might appear spiritual, we are producing wild grapes. We cause a bad smell to the community and to God. We might make it to heaven, but we lose eternal rewards and the full power of God in our lives.

Too often we Christians think about sin only in relation to eternity. Will I get into heaven or not? We might make it to heaven but sin will be judged either on earth or in eternity.

Secret sin results in tragedy for the Christian in his life on earth and his eternal rewards. Sins have serious consequences and limit or hinder us while we are on earth. Sin separates us from God. In Isaiah 64:7 we read "...for thou hast hid thy face from us...because of our iniquities" and Isaiah 59:2 "But your iniquities have separated between you and your God, and your sins have hid His face from you, that He will not hear." Our prayers are not answered when we have hidden sins in our life because God sees them. "If I regard iniquity in my heart, the Lord will not hear me." (Ps. 66:18) We are instructed in Hebrews 12:2 to "... lay aside every weight, and the sin that doth so easily beset us..." We cannot grow and mature in our spiritual lives if we hold on to sin. We will not prosper. "He that covereth his sins shall not prosper..." (Pr. 28:13) We will discover that the fruit produced while either holding sins in our heart or outwardly committing them will be like wild grapes.

For eternity the situation is also tragic. Sin can lead to an ultimate breaking of my relationship with God. This ends in eternal separation from God. Even if I still want to be a Christian but continue in disobedience through hidden sin, there are eternal consequences. "For God shall bring every work into judgment, with every secret thing, whether it be good or bad" (Ec. 12:14) and in Luke 12:2 Jesus said, "...for there is nothing covered that will not be revealed; neither hid that shall not be known." Wild grapes have no wholesome value whether they are large or tiny.

We use the term "hidden sins" but there really is no such thing to God. Secret sins will produce wild grapes. God will always see the fruit and most people will eventually notice it as well.

God told Israel that it was producing wild grapes of secret sins and impure lives. What about the Church today? Christ "gave Himself for it that He might sanctify and cleanse it with the washing of water by the Word, that He might present it to Himself a glorious church, not having spot, or wrinkle or any such thing.." He is coming back for that kind of church but we need to allow Him to prune the vines of wild grapes.

Think about it

1. We are told not to judge. How is it different to discern?

2. Does the church today serve as a model by its character and actions?

3. What actions/decisions of the church should be viewed from the aspect of being "politically correct"?

4. Does God ever answer our requests even when they are not good for us?

5. Is it okay to build large expensive churches? Why or why not?

Chapter 7

Little Wild Grapes Are Still Wild

When I was teaching first grade in a public school I had a student from a particular denomination whose parents said parties, like birthday and Valentine's Day were a sin according to the Bible. The verse they used was from Isaiah 1:14 "...your appointed feasts my soul hateth..." I had to always let them know if there was going to be a party of any sort in my classroom so she could take her son home before it started. She honestly believed she had correctly interpreted the verse but she did ignore context.. We need to beware we do not justify our beliefs by misusing Scripture to prove them.

A story is told about a Sunday School teacher who asked her class of fourth graders to define a lie. After several minutes of silence one of the boys said, "A lie is an abomination unto the Lord and a very present help in time of trouble!" Although the boy gave a Scriptural answer, he was a little confused and took verses out of context. Taking Scripture out of context is another subject altogether. We need to be careful we read what comes before and after a verse we like and see the setting etc, but we all can easily take things out of context, even when the point we are making is Biblically correct.

We like the idea that a "little white lie" is a "help in time of need." We say sometimes a lie is not really bad, but can be used to be polite or to add or exaggerate details to make a story more interesting. If it is by chance a sin it was just a "little sin." We have this list of what we consider major and minor sins.

We humans tend to rank sins by circumstances and severity of their earthly consequences. At the top are the big sins- like murder or child abuse and at the bottom are little sins like exaggerating. Some sins are just a lot more acceptable to society and to the church than others, but God doesn't rate sin like we humans do. It is true that some sins have more tragic or widespread consequences than others, but sin is sin in God's eyes. The consequences of sin in a Christian's life are wild grapes that will "poison" society and hinder are influence for Christ. If involved in sin we need to confess it and, if it affects others, we need to make it right.

In discussing hidden sins we might be quick to think of Christians who are in bondage to pornography or sexual perversions. We might think of hatred or violent anger, but there are hidden sins that create a stench to God that the world accepts as normal and sad to say some Christians do too. One of these is pride. Pride will produce wild grapes. The sin of pride is often acceptable because we use terms like self-confidence or self esteem. It is hard sometimes to distinguish the difference between proper self image and pride. If we watch the actions and reactions of people, however, the difference can be detected. Pride is an "I know best" attitude. It is unteachable and condescending toward others. It shows itself as self importance and putting on airs. This attitude can be found not only in the very capable or financially well off, but also in the average person. Pride is not actually based on value or worth but inner attitude. People who have pride like to be the center of attention and conversation. They often end up talking about their own abilities and accomplishments. I t is usually easy for us to see pride in other people, but not be aware of it in ourselves..

As I was growing up a common expression I often heard was "self praise stinketh." Self praise is a pride issue. We feel we need to impress people with our wealth, talents, or importance. It can come from an inferiority complex or from feeling superior to others. Pride is a sin not just a bad habit. God says in Proverbs 6:16, 17, "These six things doth the Lord hate; yea seven are an abomination unto him; a proud look..." The Amplified Bible describes pride - "the spirit that makes one overestimate himself and underestimate others." It is sad but many congregations and individual Christians struggle with pride and don't recognize it as such. We don't think of pride as a sin but rather as an annoying characteristic in someone else but a sense of confidence in ourselves.

In our local area we have dozens of churches within a few miles radius. There is often a spirit of competition among them. They strive to be the biggest, richest, most beautiful, have the best facilities, largest church signs, finest music, most talented people and even being the church with the best sports teams. Churches get caught up with trying to offer the best programs and the most well known speakers. Not that it is wrong for churches to strive to meet needs in the community or to have things to attract the unsaved, but these things can become a pride issue. We compete to have the largest attendance or offerings or buildings. No church is perfect. No one church can have the best programs in every area. Each church needs to meet the needs in its area and should seek God to see what He wants for its program in order to meet the needs of the people who attend it and the needs of the local community. A Church should not strive to get ahead of another church. Some churches grow in numbers, not by winning the lost, but by stealing the sheep from smaller churches, because they offer more splashy programs or facilities.

I know of a church that took great pride in the ladies who baked wonderful goodies and willingly brought them to the church's social events. A fairly new attendee offered to bring cookies for a social event, but when she took them to the church kitchen some of the ladies felt they did not measure up to their standard and so stuck them back in a corner where they could be "accidentally" overlooked and not be served. When the new lady came back at the end of the meeting she made mention of the fact that she had not seen her plate of cookies out on the serving table. The ladies acted all apologetic and looked about pretending that somehow they had gotten "lost" or overlooked. They gave her plate of cookies back to her and I still remember the puzzled and hurt look on her face. As you may guess she did not come back. I do not even know if she was saved. This act must have sent a wild grape stench to God's nostrils. We can be guilty of pride that actually hinders the ministry and primary focus of the church- loving and winning people for Jesus. It is a pride in one's reputation in the community

Besides being guilty of "place" Christians can take pride in race. We do not welcome certain ethnic or social groups that we feel are inferior to us. We are fearful of getting too many of "that kind" and maybe our children will grow up and marry somebody from that class of people. These people may be of a different color, background, race or social status. Most Christians would not admit it but that attitude exists in Christian churches. We do not want the wrong class of people to become a permanent part of **our** church. If they do come we ignore them as much as possible and inwardly hope they won't come back. We are very friendly to rich or influential people that are equal or above our social rank. We welcome them and invite them back. We figure these people of influence in the community will help give our church clout. I have been in churches where the unsaved would not be very welcome unless they were of importance in the community. We fear having people come who are gay, divorced, tattooed, smoke or drink, or have visible body piercing. We excuse this attitude by expressing our concern about what influence they will have on our young people or what the community will think if they come to our church. Our "holier than thou" atmosphere will probably keep them away.

One time a person complained to me that her church had put cans outside by the door, so smokers could leave their cigarette butts outside. Her concern was what people would think if these smokers attended her church. It might give the church a "bad name" in the community. I suggested to her that maybe she would prefer we put up a sign saying- If you smoke, leave your butt out here. The ones Jesus came to seek and to save are sometimes not welcomed in our churches by His children. When we react this way we are like the Jewish leaders who criticized Jesus for His reaching out to the needy and outcasts. The Jews saw themselves as having no needs for they were "Abraham's Seed." They did not want to touch the unclean. What are we the church afraid of? Are we afraid the world will influence us? We need to remember that greater is He that is in us than he that is in the world. We can reach our community and world for God if we allow God to deal with our pride.

Successful self-effort can also end in pride. It is all too easy to use our natural gifts, creativity, charisma and tireless efforts to create a big church. This seems to be a dangerous trend in the American church. There have been a lot of books written about church growth. These books can be helpful but also dangerous. Various church leaders have shared their methods of expanding their church. This is not necessarily wrong but if a church tries to copy or imitate a man instead of seeking God's direction and leadership, it can destroy itself. Every church and pastor has its own unique personality and gifts and should not try to imitate or attempt to model after another ministry. Books can give some practical suggestions or ideas. It might also give inspiration and encouragement to a struggling church, but when one church tries to duplicate the program of another church it can result in loss. I know of some churches where the pastor and/or board read a book and tried to copy the plan without finding what God wanted for their church. Some actually ended up destroying what they had and having to close their doors completely. Self-effort and operating by a man's plan is really pride in one's human ability. It produces wild grapes.

The last type of pride at which we will look is nationalistic pride. I don't think there can be anyone who loves and appreciates being an American and living in America more than I do. I have visited or lived in Africa, Europe, even Russia and there is no place like home, but just because I am an American and live here doesn't make me a Christian. We do have a Christian heritage in spite of those who try to deny it and we have much for which to be thankful. The day seems to be coming when Christians might not find it so easy to live in the States. It is important we pray for our nation but we must not see it as a part of our Christian faith. Some of the early worldwide mission efforts not only introduced Christianity to the unsaved but tried to turn their homes and churches into American ones. The style of music and worship needs to be unique to the people not a copy of America. America and Christianity are not synonymous. Just being born in America or into a Christian family does not make me a Christian. Corrie Ten Boom's father put it well - a mouse may **live** in a cookie jar, but it doesn't make him a cookie.

Pride in the church or in the individual Christian's life will produce wild grapes that give off a bad smell to the community. People will identify a church by calling it the "rich church" or the "elite church" or even the "country club." The unsaved will not want to come because they feel uncomfortable or fear they will not be treated well unless they meet certain standards. The unsaved should never be made to feel like they are not good enough to come to our churches.

We need to recognize a prideful attitude in ourselves and take it to the Lord. We need to be God-confident and boast in what the Lord does. We need to say with the Psalmist: "In God we boast all the day long..." and "My soul shall make her boast in the Lord..."

If we keep our focus on the Lord and what He is doing, our lives will be more fruitful and attractive to others. There are two things we will stop being as soon as we know we are- the one is deceived and the other is **humble.**

We have looked at various sins that may seem small to us but we need to remember that with God all sin is sin and he doesn't weigh the sin to see how bad it is. He does not have a grading system for sin, even though many times we do.

Pride is one of these sins we often do not look upon as big sin, but pride in any form is sin and can have serious consequences for us and other people.

Does God see any wild grapes in my life or in my church? Does He speak this parable of the Vineyard to us as He did to Israel? Let us repent and be the person and church God wants us to be, not too good for someone in need to stay away from or to try to make our church a carbon copy of another.

Today many churches have replaced true worship with entertainment and relationship with Christ with organization.

Perhaps we sometimes forget that the head of the church is Jesus Christ and we are just the "keepers" not the owners. We need to seek His face and do what He wants for our church and do it in His way and His strength. When we do this the results will be twofold- we will experience the abundant fruitful life and the fruit produced will make the world hungry for the God we have.

Think about it

1. Is there ever a time when we should tell a lie?

2. Are some sins more serious than others? If so what sins?

3. What is the difference between pride and self esteem?

4. Can low self esteem be a sin?

5. Do you know any churches that followed the plan of a man's book on church growth? What was the result?

Chapter 8

What Makes Bitter Fruit?

A local pastor once told me that he had been criticized by many individuals in his years of ministry. I do not doubt that at all, because we Christians are all too willing to find fault with pastoral leadership. Many people demand perfection from their pastor and define perfection according to their personal agenda. This particular pastor had been criticized for preaching too long, too short, reading too much Scripture, not reading enough Scripture etc. His response was to save all these written criticisms and to read over them again and again reliving the hurt he had felt. This can lead to self-pity resentment and bitterness. All too many pastors have been criticized to the point where they leave the ministry or build up frustrations that can lead to anger and bitterness.

Deuteronomy 32:32 mentions bitter grape clusters. Just before his death, Moses was given a prophetic type of song from God. In this song he tells of the goodness and holiness of God's character in contrast to the wicked character of Israel. He reminds Israel of all God had done for them and how God had delivered them and fed them with "butter and curds and milk" and with the "finest of the wheat" and drink "of the blood of the grape." In response to God's blessings Israel had "provoked Him to jealousy with strange gods." He continues by reminding them that God would "spurn" and "reject" them and "hide His face" from them. He through Moses warns them that He would allow their enemies to triumph over them. Then God actually denounces these enemies because they do not serve God either and that their vine comes from sinful roots. In fact the enemies' vines produce bitter clusters. The day will come when God will wreak vengeance upon them. Bitter grapes are hated by God and those who produce them will be punished.

The Hebrew root word for bitter as it is used here means acrid and poisonous. The root word is used in various forms and can carry the idea of snake venom. This form of the word is used only one other place in Scripture. Job used it when he complained to God that God had written bitter things against him, because of his iniquities as a youth.

More commonly the form used for bitterness carries the idea of vexation or being bitterly provoked. This form of the word is used more than a dozen times in the Old Testament. This form is used by Isaiah when he speaks not really of bitter grapes but of bitter wine. In Isaiah 24:9 Isaiah tells the Israelites that they will not drink wine with singing, but that the wine will be bitter. He warns the people that they will experience vexation because of their idol worship.

This same root form of the word for bitter used in Isaiah is found in the book of Ruth. In the first chapter of Ruth we read that Naomi had gone with her husband and sons into Moab, because of the famine in Israel. While there her sons married women of Moab. Naomi's husband and two sons died, and she returned to Israel with the one daughter-in-law Ruth. Upon her arrival she told the people not to call her Naomi (meaning pleasantness) but to call her Mara (bitter). She told how God had dealt bitterly with her. That is to say God angered and provoked her.

As I stated before it is important to understand that Old Testament Jews did not understand how satan worked. They believed that all things came from God- both good and evil. They had little understanding of satan, because their knowledge of Scripture was limited to only a few of the Old Testament books. I believe that God did not reveal more about satan to the Old Testament believers in order to protect them. If they had understood more of satan they would have lived in fear for he was the prince of this world before Jesus' death and resurrection.

While Jesus was on earth He began to show His power over satan. Jesus sent out the seventy. He gave them power over satan:

> "Behold, I give unto you power (authority) to tread on serpents and scorpions and over all the power (ability) of the **enemy.**" (Lk. 10:19)

Notice the two different Greek meanings of the English word power. This can be understood easily if we think of a policeman or road workman who wants to stop traffic. He does not have the **power (ability)** to stop any cars on his own physical ability. The driver could run into him and knock him over and to keep on going forward, but that policeman or worker has the **power (ability/authority)** to stop cars, because of his position and the government of the state behind him. That is how it is with us. We do not have the ability within us to stop satan, but because of our position in Christ and all of heaven behind us we do not **need** to let satan run over us. We need to understand that. It is sad that we too often let satan control us and give in to His temptations.

This **ability** became ours when Jesus died. At the death of Jesus:

> "...that through death he might destroy him that had the power of death, that is, the devil." (Heb. 2:14)

> "...now shall the prince of this world be cast out" (Jn. 12:31)

As Jesus was about to die on the cross he said this about satan:

> "Now is the judgment of this world; now shall the prince of this world be cast out." (Jn. 12:31)

and at the resurrection of Jesus He triumphed over satan:

> "...having spoiled principalities and powers, He made a shew of them openly, triumphing over them..." (Col. 2:15

This is even clearer in the Amplified Bible:

> "God **disarmed** the principalities and powers that were ranged against us and made a bold display and public example of them, in triumphing over them in Him and in it (Cross)"

satan lost his position as prince of this world. That is the New Testament understanding of satan, and our standing before him covered by the blood of Christ. That's why we put on our armor, so that when satan comes at us he is not sure who is inside.

When Paul was before Agrippa he proclaimed he had been sent to the Gentiles to "open their eyes, and to turn them from darkness to light, and from the power of satan unto God." (Acts 26:15-18) This was the message of the New Testament:

> "For this purpose the Son of God was manifested that he might destroy the works of the devil." (I Jn. 38)

We are told satan was defeated. Although he will continue to harass us and tempt us, we know the day is coming when we will see him utterly and finally defeated:

> "And then shall that Wicked be revealed, whom the Lord shall consume with the spirit of his mouth and shall destroy..." (II Th. 2:8)

This was not the position of satan in the Old Testament nor was it possible for humans to defeat satan in the same way. They remained spiritually dead without the Holy Spirit to indwell their sinful body for the sacrifices of blood only covered sin. It did not remove it like the sacrificial blood of Jesus does today. Therefore God could not give them a complete understanding of satan. That is why we find when Moses wrote the history of the Children of Israel that he stated that God hardened Pharaoh's heart. God does not do an evil thing like making people hard, however He allows us to make choices which can make us hard of heart and closed to Him when we reject His truth.

Pharaoh made the choice of refusing to see God's work. In those days, just as in these days, people had a will and God allows people to make a choice. We need to be reminded again of how limited the knowledge of satan's power and activities is without the New Testament writings. I discovered a number of things in the Old Testament that made more sense to me after I heard the testimony of a Messianic Jew who got caught up in demonic activities to find success and happiness in life without realizing the origin of the supernatural power available through the cult. He said Jewish people feel and have always felt all good as well as evil came from the hand of God.

This helps us understand why Naomi blamed God for the bad things that had happened to her family. It was not God's plan to have Elimelech and Naomi move to Moab. There is no record of their asking God what to do about the famine that was upon them. When Naomi and her family moved into Moab, they dwelt in the enemy's camp. (Moab had always been an enemy to Israel) Instead of trusting God or even asking God, it would appear that Elimelech and Naomi took their family and ran in fear. This lack of trust in God's protection and provision opened them to satan's attack. God was not guilty of doing evil. God does not harm or kill His children. He is redemptive. We read God's promise that "every good gift and perfect gift is from above" (James 1:17)

Sickness and death are a result of man's original sin. We are born with a sin nature and thus susceptible to diseases and eventual death, but disobedience opens us to diseases and problems and also enables satan to attack people by causing disease. That was true for Naomi and is still true for us today. God warns us in His word:

> "He that diggeth a pit shall fall into it; and whoso breaketh an hedge, a serpent shall bite him." (Ecc. 10:8)

When we rebel or disobey God we make a weak spot for satan to attack.

It was not the will of God for the family to go to Moab. I believe God would have provided for them in Bethlehem. (Remember Moab started as a people from an act of incest and always hated God's people.) When Naomi's family got out of God's will for their lives troubles came. When we do that same thing, it is easy to become bitter and blame God for our problems. When difficult things come into our lives we need to be sure not to become bitter toward God. Rather we need to examine our lives to be sure to repent of any disobedience and then trust God as we walk through the problem, knowing He is able to deliver.

Of course not all difficulties are a result of our personal sin or disobedience. We need to remember that we live in a fallen world where even nature itself has been twisted by sin. We are all susceptible to nature's disasters. However we have the promises of God that He will take care of us. Jesus told His disciples:

> "...in this world ye shall have tribulation, but be of good cheer, I have overcome the world." (Jn. 16:33)

We need to be sure we do not stop reading after the word "tribulation." If we do not have an understanding of God and the world we can get upset with our lives and angry toward God giving a root of bitterness. That is what happened to Naomi.

However, at that time in history Naomi was blameless in her bitterness, because God knew she had limited knowledge, just as Job did. That was why Naomi and Job were blameless in their words against God. Remember God found no fault in Job either even though at times he seemed to speak harshly against God. God has a higher standard for His children today because we have more revelation knowledge. Today we still have opportunities for bitterness and anger in our lives, but God has revealed it as sin and made provision to forgive and remove it. We need to ask God to do that. We do not need to let resentment and anger build up within us. Bitterness toward God and others will eventually erupt into anger in words and/or actions.

When I was in college, I joined the debate team. I guess I have always liked to talk. As we would organize our arguments to defend our position, sometimes we would see a weak point. When we presented a weak argument another member of the team liked to say - point is weak, say it louder and maybe pound the podium. I have noticed preachers doing that. I remember the days of preaching when pulpits were pounded for emphasis. Today many pastors and preachers have struggled with bitterness and anger and we as their parishioners have possibly added to that. Sometimes when the pulpit is pounded today, you get the feeling it was done because the preacher had had an argument with his wife or family before he got to church or is upset with his flock. At times I think it might have been stressed loudly because the man was frustrated and angry with the criticism of his church and his own faults and frustrations in his own life.

Recently I heard a psychologist talking on how to avoid anger. He pointed out to us that anger is not the root of our exploding, but the result of other deeper issues in life. It may be bitterness or a rejection. Many times we feel it is an attack on us personally or an attack on our character, where we have a fault or weakness.

We all have faults and it is so easy to see those same faults in others and become impatient or angry with them. I remember a certain student I had who really annoyed me at times. I asked another teacher if she saw that annoying habit in that student in her classes. I was surprised, but also enlightened, when she pointed out that I was annoyed because I had the same bad habit in my life! I recalled a statement which my psychology professor often said- we see things not as **they are** but as **we are**. It is easy to get upset with people who act like we do. We see our own weaknesses and find them very annoying in others. We can become angry and bitter. Sometimes we are angry because the church expects us, as members, to follow certain rules or standards. The more conservative and legalistic churches usually have a long list of do's and don't's. An older Christian who is in bondage to rules can see a young Christian enjoying freedom in Christ. This causes resentment and he feels bitter because he watches the younger Christian enjoying things that he was taught were wrong although not Biblically prohibited. This will produce bitter grapes.

In the New Testament we are warned against being bitter:

"Let all bitterness, and wrath, and anger, and clamour, and evil speaking, be put away from you..." (Eph. 4:31)

In Greek the words for bitter are derived from a root word which carries the idea of something sharp and piercing. Bitterness will lead to anger and usually end in isolation from others. The book of Hebrews talks about a "root of bitterness." In this section the writer is dealing with God's chastening of His children. We need to understand that the word for chastening as it is used here is a positive action - one of training or bringing up by instructing, not beating and abuse. God does correct us but He does not do it by diseases and tragedies. It is true however that if we do not respond positively to His correction, it opens us up to problems and to satanic attacks. God chastens us through our soul and spirit not our bodies. He speaks to us through His Word. In John 15:3 Jesus said, "Now ye are clean through the Word..." This means not only are we made clean but also God uses the Word to show us where we need to be made clean. Jesus in His prayer in John17:17 prayed, "Sanctify them through thy truth, thy word is truth." Unlike some human parents, God always disciplines in love, never out of anger or frustration. No loving human parents would give their children cancer or diseases or purposely cause an accident to cripple or harm them. Only perverted people would do that. So how can we imagine God would treat His disobedient child in that manner? When we refuse to amend our ways, however, satan gets a foothold in our life and brings bad things. God will use that harmful thing to continue to admonish us.

Even though God's discipline is loving and perfect, it can still be hard on us emotionally. He may ask us to do things that are out of our comfort zone or to stop doing things that we depend on for our "comfort blanket." If we feel that obedience will cause us pain, we might delay making the change or just refuse to change. By our refusal we will experience greater pain and can develop an anger toward God, creating a "root of bitterness." Our bitterness and anger make us strike out at others and we become sharp and piercing. Continued disobedience often makes us judgmental and critical. I believe there are many Christians, as well as the unsaved, that have this problem. This is why today we have a problem known as road rage and frustrated angry people who go on shooting sprees. The world can't help itself, but we Christians have Someone who can help us deal with frustration and anger because we can know we are loved.

Sometimes anger erupts when we are corrected because we have allowed bitterness to build a stronghold in us. Even when we are corrected by God we can respond in anger or repentance. The writer of Hebrews tells us how to accept correction from God by looking beyond the discipline itself to see the positive results of accepting it. In Hebrews 12:11-15 he admits that discipline although not joyous ends in positive consequences because it "... yields a harvest of peaceful and righteous fruit (grapes?), conforms us to God's will, results in right living and right standing with God." (Amp)

Christians need to realize any one of us can make poor choices and sin. We are a "body" of believers and should be encouraging and healing toward each other. We all will experience God's correction at times, but like the body we need to sympathize and help bring healing not chop off the arm or leg or keep poking at the wound. I heard someone say that the only army that shoots its wounded and hurting is the church.

It is easy when we are suffering to make excuses for hurting others. What did Jesus do when he was paying the supreme price of obedience-the death on the cross? He was in torment physically, emotionally and spiritually. Yet He looked down from the cross and instructed John to take care of His mother! This is an amazing kindness shown to someone in the midst of agony. There was no root of bitterness in Christ as He died for us. He was able to see other people's needs, even the men crucified next to Him.

God may speak to us directly through the Word or through an inner voice, but He may also use a Christian brother or sister to come to talk to us about a problem in our lives. This correction needs to be done only if God instructs us to do it and that it must be done in love.

When we fail to submit to discipline, whether from God or another Christian, we can develop bitterness through unforgiveness. Sometimes it can be a result of another person hurting us deliberately or unintentionally. We live in a world of all kinds of people and personality types. Some folks are just by temperament more gentle and loving and easy to get along with, but others who are more blunt can hurt our feelings. When we are hurt by someone it is easy to keep reliving the scene over and over- rehearsing the "he said' or "she said" lines. This only allows resentment to build and hinders forgiveness.

God deals with us in forgiveness. There are times when we have cried out to God in our anger and blamed Him for letting it happen or even making it happen, but He forgives when we ask Him because He knows our lack of understanding and immature behavior. It is like a small child getting angry with his parent.

When I was in high school I use to babysit for a doctor's family to make money to put toward my college costs. One day I had been with the children while their mother was out. Around supper time she came home and I was getting ready to leave. The one little girl Nanette was about 5 years old and she was hungry. Her mother was starting supper and Nanette asked for a cookie. Mother said, "No, we're going to eat supper in a little while." Nanette asked again with a little more whine in her voice but was told "no" again. At this point Nanette in her frustration and anger said, "I hate you! I don't want to live here anymore! I want to go home with Sharon. She'll give me a cookie." I know that response was not pleasing to her mother, but I also know her mother understood she did not mean it, but said it out of anger and frustration. Nanette was just immature. That is all right for a five year old. It will soon be forgiven and forgotten. However if a 20-year-old acts that way it is much more hurtful and serious.

This illustrates a spiritual lesson for us. If we are immature, a young Christian, and we get angry with God, He understands we are still children. He forgives and forgets. If we have been a Christian for years and still get angry toward God it is more serious and grieves God more. Yet God always forgives when we come in repentance.

I have served in several different Christian ministries and taught in Christian schools and have received my share of criticism- some justly but many unjustly. The Lord had to teach me to listen carefully or read the letters carefully and prayerfully and then if there was truth in them to make adjustments or corrections, but if not then forget them and throw the letters away and not hold unforgiveness in my heart. We can learn from people correcting us, even if it is not always done in love, but we need to forget the tone or manner of correction and ask God's help to change and then forgive and forget. Remembering exact words or tone of voice can lead to inability to forgive and give opportunity for a root of bitterness to form.

One time I had a conversation with an adult lady that was unhappy with our pastor. The pastor liked teasing people in fun but had not learned that some people do not know how to take things he said. They were not really insulting but just jokes. Anyway one day shortly after he had come to our church he asked this lady a question about how everyone in her family was doing. He then made a remark about all family's having a few nuts in their family tree or something like that. She became very angry and walked away. When I talked to her about it she claimed he knew she had a relative in a mental institution and he was belittling her. I am sure he did not know that or he would not have made an offhand remark like that because he really was a very loving caring man. Anyway this lady had let this build up in her until it became a root of bitterness and then found it easy to find fault and criticize many of the pastor's words and actions. When she told me about this she was complaining about another statement he had made from the pulpit that if people were not happy in our church they could leave. This was true. There were a number of people who continually complained and talked about all the changes he had made and how they didn't like it. He had later in public asked the congregation to forgive him. He had not meant to be so blunt. Anyway she wanted me to know I should try to help get rid of this troublemaker. When I reminded her he had asked forgiveness for the statement she told me she could not forgive him. She had allowed let a root of bitterness to spring up in her that was going to do more damage to her than to others.

Sometimes it might be hard to forget but we can choose to forgive. Remember Jesus taught us "forgive us our trespasses as we forgive those who trespass against us."

It is understandable that unsaved people may be unable to forgive and hold bitterness. They will use their tongues to gossip, curse, spread poison and deal treacherously with others. In describing the unsaved man Paul wrote this:

> "Their throat is an open sepulchre; with their tongues they have used deceit; the poison of asps is under their lips; whose mouth is full of cursing and bitterness." (Rom. 3:13, 14)

How sad when we find Christians behaving the same way. It is an offense against God. It can destroy another person's reputation and character. It can divide and destroy families and can split and destroy the ministry of a pastor and church.

The Apostle Paul wrote this admonition:

> "Let all bitterness and indignation and wrath(passion, rage, bad temper) and resentment(anger, animosity) and quarreling (brawling, clamor, contention) and slander(evil speaking, abusive or blasphemous language) be banished from you, with all malice(spite, ill will, or baseness of any kind)." (Eph. 4:31 Amp)

Another root of bitterness can spring up through jealousy. Too often we as Christians compete with one another and excuse it as working for the Lord. We do need to use our gifts and abilities, but we need to remember they come from God and He has a time and place for us to use them. We do not need to compete to be better than others. This really is a form of pride and produces wild grapes, as well as bitter ones. There is no verse that tells us it is a sin to compete, but when we are competing we are actually comparing ourselves to others and there is Scripture that tells us comparing is not wisdom:

> "Not that we...compare ourselves with some who exalt and furnish testimonials for themselves! However when they measure themselves with themselves and compare themselves with one another, they are without understanding and behave unwisely." (II Cor. 10:12, Amp)

The reason it is not wise to compare with one another is because it is sure to result in sin. Either we become proud or we feel inferior and become jealous. God has given us the gifts He wants us to use. A list of these basic gifts can be found in Romans 12. Before Paul describes the gifts, he reminds us that we are to present our bodies as a living sacrifice and not to think of ourselves more highly because these gifts are really God's and we are to use them for His work. We had no say when we were born as to which gift(s) we wanted. God did the choosing. It is important that we discover the gift(s) God has given us. Too many people say they can't do anything of value. Others don't know what their gift is and they get involved with a ministry for which they are not gifted. I have seen it in churches that I have attended. For example someone thinks they have a gift of teaching but they have a gift of mercy or organization. Then they wonder why they are not asked to teach and if they volunteer the class is not learning as they should and sometimes gets smaller. If they are mistaken in what they think their gift is, they may be teaching a class that God has for another individual with the gift of teaching. When people get in the wrong place of a church's ministry, it can create problems.

One of the problems in understanding gifts is the confusion between those described in Romans 12 and I Corinthians 12. The gifts of Romans 12 are given to us to use as we choose. I have seen over the years that everyone, Christian or unsaved, has one or more of the gifts named in Romans 12. The problem is that the unsaved use them in perverted ways, e.g. the gift of mercy can be used to protect animals and trees and yet abort babies. However the gifts of I Corinthians12 are not available to the unsaved, except as demonic counterfeits. They are for Christians to use personally or for the church through the Holy Spirit "Who apportions to each person individually (exactly) as He chooses." The use of any of these gifts can lead to competing and jealousy if we do not know who we are in Christ. Not knowing my God given gift, serving in the wrong position and comparing myself with others can create bitter grapes.

There is one more wrong attitude held by too many Christians and found in too many churches- tradition and legalism and they are preserved to some degree in almost every denomination and church. I am not talking about the individuals who want to hold to a strong Biblical theology, but rather hold on to traditions of the church because they have been a part of church life so long that they do not understand the difference between traditions and Scripture.

We have looked at bitter grapes. The root of bitterness results in jealousy, anger and resentment. We see examples of this not only in churches today but recorded in Scripture. Joseph's brothers were jealous of him and this developed into hatred toward Joseph. Saul was jealous of David and began to despise him. The Jewish leaders resented Jesus' teaching, authority and popularity and hated Him. We could give many examples of people who allow jealousy and bitterness to lead to hatred and bitter grapes.

Perhaps one of the most tragic examples from Scripture with long lasting and continued bitterness and hatred that has been passed down for generations is the one recorded in Genesis between Esau and Jacob. Esau despised his birthright and so he had to serve his younger brother, contrary to Jewish culture and tradition. Esau then lost his firstborn Abrahamic blessing. Esau then married the daughter of another "outcast" Ishmael. (Gen. 28:9) Esau had a son Eliphaz who was father to Amalek. (Gen. 36:12) This root of bitterness and jealousy was passed down to a whole nation of the Amalekites who hated the Jews and the Edomites later known as Idumeans, which produced the Herods. The Agagites also hated the Jews and Agag was the king of the Amalekites. Later we read in the book of Esther about a man named Haman who hated Mordecai and the Jews and is called an Agagite - probably related to the Amalekites and Ishmael and Esau.

A year or two ago I was given a book by a friend. It was a great book and very enlightening to me. It was written by a converted Muslim named Faisal Malick. The title was *Here Comes Ishmael.* In this writing he traces the Islamic people to Ishmael and Esau. He states that the terrorist group of Muslims comes from Esau, and the spirit of Esau is what causes Islamic terrorism. It is an interesting book that every Christian should read. This spirit that dominates many Muslims is from the root of bitterness of Esau.

Although we might ignore bitterness in our lives thinking nothing serious will result from it, we are ignoring the possible far reaching consequences. We may not create national conflicts but we might destroy another individual or family, or ministry. Bitterness is a contagious sin. No one can afford to allow himself to be a vine that produces bitter grapes. If we are producing bitter grapes in our lives we need to seek God and take care of the deep underlying reason for it. Bitterness does not come from a branch that is intimately connected to the Vine.

Think about it

1. Has someone provoked or offended you? How did you or how are you dealing with it?

2. Do you deal differently with a non-Christian than a Christian who hurts you?

3. Did Jesus ever have opportunity to be hurt, vexed or offended with others? How did He deal with it?

4. Is there any place for competition in the church or between churches? When?

5. Can you think of someone who is not a Christian who has an inborn gift from the list in Romans 12? Explain it.

6. Do you see these Roman 12 gifts in others at church? What should you do about it?

Chapter 9

Bitter Fruit is not Worth Preserving

Although I started attending church when I was in fifth grade and I found the Bible stories and facts interesting, it did not change my everyday life. The church was in a small rural town and had very deep family roots. I think if you went back enough generations you could have started a family tree and put everyone who attended the church on a branch connected to another. One of our neighbors who didn't attend this church once said she never spoke an unkind word about any person in that church to another person because they would somehow be related. The adults were very kind and loving. The young people were friendly on a surface level but we didn't really get involved in their activities outside of church for a number of years. I think there were several reasons for this. For one we were outsiders and they felt we were different from them. We probably appeared to be more "citified" because we had more store bought clothes, even though my mother was a good seamstress and did hand make many of our clothes and home furnishings. We also had indoor plumbing and many of them didn't. I was not aware of this feeling until a few years later when we became better friends.

Another reason, which I mentioned earlier, was the fact that I was eager to hear what was said in church. It was all new to me, so I sat up front with adults but the other young people sat in the back and passed around pictures and notes because they had heard it all before.

Perhaps the last reason we felt like outsiders was that we were baby Christians. The church we attended was very strong on teaching separation from the world. At school I wasn't very "separated." I was not the shy sweet Christian that the others from that church were. I think they were embarrassed to be associated with me. I can't blame them for that because some of my friends were not the best influence on me.

The church denomination belonged to what was called the National Holiness Association and had a lot of "thou shalt nots." I didn't! Although I had gone to the altar in the front of the church during an evangelistic meeting when I was about twelve and wanted to be a Christian, I really didn't understand much about what that meant. I didn't know anything about the Christian walk. In fact after I went forward I felt embarrassed because I thought I had done something silly. Now I realize it was satan telling me that but at that time I just half wished I hadn't done it. My life was really no different than it had been before and I had no concept of how to grow spiritually. In the summer between my ninth and tenth grade of high school my life did change. The deacon couple that had so faithfully picked us up every Sunday and taken us to church with them offered to pay for a week at a Christian camp. While there I made a serious commitment to the Lord and I learned more about what it meant to be a Christian and my life changed.

Along with that commitment came a decision to be the best Christian I could be, but I still had more head knowledge than heart understanding. As I said the church denomination I was attending was somewhat legalistic in outward dress and activities. Although I must admit they did not try to force them on me. However I picked up the attitudes and ideas and traditions of the people there and became very legalistic about a lot of things. I wanted to be accepted and be like those people who had brought me to the Lord and so I adopted all the church traditions as Biblical truths. To be like them and be accepted as one of them I felt I had to be even more stubborn and determined to do the "Christian" traditions.

I was learning all the facts but not the secret of being a fruitful Christian. I was not told that the fruit of the spirit is in us when we are born again and there are ways to develop and grow in spirit. Just learning Biblical facts does not develop fruit.

Reading and memorizing Scripture are good things to do, but that does not make me necessarily mature or fruitful or even a Christian. There are people in prison who can quote Scripture. We remember that satan himself can do that. He used it to tempt Jesus. Of course he did take it out of context. We can have a knowledge of the Bible without fruit. Knowledge is not a fruit of the spirit and won't even produce fruit. In fact knowledge leads to pride and that is what took place in my life. I knew facts but lacked wisdom and understanding of revelation knowledge or recognizing when God speaks personally. I was busy doing and trying to act holy but was only gaining soul knowledge and not developing in spirit. A revelation understanding of God's Word does not come from education or from the head. It comes to the spirit. We need soul knowledge but it must not stop there. I began doing and not doing the things that marked me as a Christian by my church's regulations. It led me into a superior attitude because in our church we didn't do certain things like smoke, drink, go to movies, dance, or listen to certain kinds of music and didn't hang around with those that did. I could argue the evils of such things with anyone.

This attitude stayed with me through my time at our church college and into my first year of teaching when I had a shock but a learning experience. I was teaching first and second graders in a one room school. One of my boys named Brad came from a Christian home and I knew he loved Jesus. Every day when he came to school he had to bring me a treat for lunch- a homemade goody, piece of fruit or a picture. One day he told me his mother was a hairdresser. I could not understand how a woman could be a Christian and a hairdresser. Yet when I met her and the family I knew they had to be Christians. It was the first opening of my eyes to see beyond my narrow world of traditional ideas about what it meant to be Christian. I still had a long way to go but God was beginning to teach me the difference between traditions and Bible truths.

Everybody has certain traditions, rituals or habits that have become important to them. This is not necessarily a bad thing. Traditions can give stability to life and even bring great joy. Some traditions can be very meaningful and helpful to us as Christians, but others could simply mean we are in a rut. In fact traditions can sometimes limit us and hinder others. It is important that we recognize the difference between tradition and Biblical directives and principles.

Bitter grapes of tradition can be found preserved on the vine with a "Do Not Pick" sign. The religious traditions become exactly that- religious. They become the sacred cows of whole churches and denominations. Individuals within these groups will obstinately defend them even to the point of trying to prove they are Biblical. This is what I label "religion." They believe there is only one way to do something and get upset and indignant toward others who do not conform, because they consider these traditions as correct Biblical behavior and practice. Religion comes into power when it is a **choice** that is forced upon others rather than a **Biblical command.**

We can get into a maintaining mode. We want to keep the past alive. That is not necessarily bad because we do need to maintain our Biblical integrity, but we need to know what and why we are maintaining something. I recently read a statement by a man named Gaston Bachelard, "One must always maintain one's connection to the past and yet ceaselessly pull away from it." We need to remember our past with loving memories, but also be willing to move on to new concepts and methods that are God given. We are made in God's image and therefore are creative and should avoid staying in a rut just because it is comfortable and familiar.

I used the term "second generation" Christians. Many Christians are in reality fourth and fifth generation. They grew up in the church doing certain things and are really in bondage to methods of church worship. They are content (not always joyful) with the way things have always been. **Religion** controls the way people should or should not worship. If a newer (should we say first generation?) Christian or even a visitor (saved or unsaved) comes to the church and does not fully conform, we feel compelled to correct or instruct them, causing confusion and strife. If we are questioned as to why a certain tradition is practiced we will either ignore the question or take Scripture out of context. An example of this is related to women wearing pant suits. I was once told it was sinful to do that. The verse used is from Deuteronomy 22:5:

> "The woman shall not wear that which pertaineth unto a man, neither shall a man put on a woman's garment: for all that do so are abomination unto the Lord thy God."

If that verse were talking about style of clothing then the men in the church today should wear robes like the men at that time. Also we should keep the rest of the rules in that chapter including verse 11 that says clothing of different blends should not be worn. We need to understand the context of that chapter of giving advice on how to avoid perverted behavior.

People can become legalistically bound by taking a verse and making a theology out of it. Then what is worse adopting it not even as a tradition but a Biblical command. When we do this it causes confusion. The second generation people are sincere in what they believe but can offend or cause strife among church members, and drive away the next generation and new Christians. This can also make unsaved people uncomfortable, even embarrassed and keep them from coming back to church.

As I look back I can remember several incidents in which I was made to feel embarrassed by "mature" Christians who thought they were instructing me in Biblical holiness, but were actually trying to force me into a traditional pattern of men. One weekend I went along with a friend from college to visit her church. They were having special services with a visiting evangelist. In the middle of his sermon he talked about the worldly practice of wearing white shoes. That was a new concept to me and I looked around up and down the few benches where I could see feet and realized that I was the only one in sight wearing my "sinful" white shoes. The next comment was on the sin of women cutting their hair and again I realized I was the only one in the church with cut hair. Needless to say I was very embarrassed feeling like everyone was looking at this wicked woman in church.

Man-made traditions can bring bondage and sometimes anger or discouragement and create strife in the home between parents and children and strife in the church because there is no source for what is being taught- only historical church life. Sometimes it causes dissension between the older and newer members of a church.

I happen to be a first generation Christian and for many years felt sorry that I did not have a Christian heritage. In fact I felt envious of those who did. It is true that there are many advantages to being born into a long line of Christians, but there are some dangers. I have learned in more recent years that I have a number of advantages. I do not have all the hang-ups and bondages that some have who have been in the church for generations. The ones that I adopted not knowing they were traditions, but thinking they were Biblical principles, I began to see more clearly. With the study of Bible I was able to differentiate between what is Biblical theology and what is man's tradition. I know many second generation Christians who are free and vibrant in the Lord, who are open to learn and grow in an intimate relationship daily, but sad to say I have also met with others who are not and who feel no fervent joy but rather feel comfortable looking at the bygone days and trying to live in them. This leads them into the "But we always did it this way" complex. It creates legalistic Christianity which is offensive to the world. The problem is that when they were growing up they apparently were not taught the difference between traditions of the church and Biblical

Not only legalistic traditions of outward dress and appearance but the manner or mode used in church observances can create disagreement, for example the way to baptize. The principle of baptism is Scriptural but the mode is not. Should it be outdoors in a stream? Jesus was baptized that way! Is it advisable for a church to have an indoor baptistery? Do we immerse or sprinkle? If we immerse, should it be once or three times and should it be forward or backward? Should it be done immediately after one accepts Christ? These kinds of "mode" beliefs have split churches or created disunity among congregations and denominations. I know a church that baptized in a swimming pool in their community. That would surely be considered heretical to some churches!

Music is another factor that has created havoc and disunity in churches. Do we use hymnbooks or overhead? Traditional hymns or newer choruses? What about instruments? Surely not drums! And on and on it goes. How does God see us while we are arguing about how to worship and don't ever really worship as a corporate body, because someone is upset about the music being sung? Often those who are bound by tradition have the concept of keeping the church pure and holy but act in an unholy manner to enforce these traditions.

Another interesting problem came up in a church that I once attended and it had to do with communion. Communion is a celebration of a covenant - the blood covenant of Christ. As we celebrate it we should be focused on the blessings that we receive through the shed blood of Christ. The elements of communion are only symbols of the New Testament covenant, but many Christians insist on making it a traditional ritualistic unchangeable ceremony. It **must always** be exactly the same! Some members of the church were very upset because our pastor changed the set pattern of passing the bread and cups back through the pews, and had each communicant come forward and break off a piece of bread from a loaf of bread and the loaf was not unleavened. This caused friction because not only was the bread to be unleavened but it had to be made from the recipe that had been passed down from generations and should have five prick points to symbolize the five wounds of Jesus. They pointed out that in Scripture Jesus used unleavened bread so we must also do it that way. Jesus probably used unleavened bread but the Greek word for bread can refer to unleavened bread or leavened bread and if it needed to be unleavened bread to please God I think Scripture would make that clear. Also Jesus probably used wine and we always used grape juice. When mention of that fact was made, it was ignored because that issue was of no importance. We had a heritage of total abstinence from alcohol. We were not doing everything just like Jesus did, but the unleavened bread was a tradition that we were not to ignore. That is the problem with confusing Scripture and tradition.

While I was living in Zimbabwe, Africa and teaching at our church mission school we would periodically celebrate not only communion but the washing of feet like Jesus did with His disciples. We read the account of Jesus washing the disciples' feet in John 13. When Jesus had finished this task He said to His disciples:

> "If I then your Lord and Master, have washed your feet; ye also ought to was one another's feet. For I have given you an example...the servant is not greater than His Lord...if ye know these things, happy are ye if ye do them." (John 13:14 - 17)

I do not think washing feet is a Biblical command. Jesus did say we are happy if we do it, but what did He mean by "it"? The Amplified Bible uses the phrase for "it" as "if you act accordingly and really do them." What Jesus did at the time was to show humility. He did the task expected of the lowest servant in the house. There are churches today that practice the actual washing of feet. I personally have been in churches that practiced that ritual and I think it is a nice symbolic action reminding us to serve others. However that does not necessarily make one humble. When Christ was on earth, the people there walked long distances and their feet actually got hot and dusty and it was the kind thing for the host or hostess to have their lowest servant wash the feet of visitors. I had been at feet washing services in the States. When we did it in the African church I was not surprised. However it came to have a whole new meaning because the African Christians had walked a long distance to get to church and their feet were hot and dirty. Many of them had no shoes to wear. For a white person to wash the feet of the black person showed humility and love and most of the white Europeans would have refused to serve in that way. The whites considered themselves above the blacks. Whites had black servants to do the menial tasks. But getting back to traditional rituals, when I did it in the African church I was told that I had to take off my sweater or button it up because Scripture says Jesus "laid aside His outer garments", so if I buttoned my sweater it was not an outer garment but if I didn't button it, it was an outer garment and had to be laid aside. I do not know where that "tradition" came from but I figured it must have come from the early American missionaries caught up with tradition.

It is easy to emphasize and be literal about certain things but lose the focus and real meaning of what the action or ritual is really about. Washing feet was a symbolic act to show I am a servant to my fellow Christian and not superior or above him, and communion is the celebration of God's covenant and promised Scriptural blessings. Communion isn't just a Sunday morning ritual but a celebration of living our whole lives under the blessings of God, not only for salvation but also for the meeting of every need of my life- spirit, soul and body. It would take another whole booklet to study all that is involved with covenant living, but that is what communion celebrates. It is not about the time or frequency of communion or the place or even the elements themselves. It is a reminder of a covenant established between the Father and Son. The study of covenants shows us that a covenant made between two individuals is a lifelong one and passes down from generation to generation. That is why David had his servants look for Mephibosheth who was the son of Jonathan. David had made a covenant with Jonathan and those promises covered the next generation. We Christians are the benefactors of promises between Jesus and His heavenly Father. We need to celebrate and focus on the covenant not the symbols.

It reminds me of an event recorded in Judges 8. After Gideon had successfully defeated Israel's enemies, some of the people wanted to make him king. He refused but asked the men to bring him the gold earrings they had taken from their enemies. With this jewelry Gideon made an ephod. The ephod was a vest like garment originally worn by the high priest. It had twelve stones in it, one for each of the tribes of Israel to remind the high priest of his responsibility to seek God for all of Israel. It had to do with the whole lifestyle and purpose of the priesthood. It was the visible reminder of all God had promised the Jewish people. Later it was worn by others, including David when he was seeking God's wisdom and direction. In verse 27 of Judges 8 we read, "...all Israel went a whoring after it; which thing became a snare..." The making of the ephod was not a sin but it became a type of god itself rather than a symbol of God's divine help and provision. It became an idol to the people because they focused on the symbol rather than God.

God also gave Israel the Ark of the Covenant as a visual symbol of His presence with them, but Israel began to look at the Ark itself as protection and victory rather than focusing on God. In I Samuel 3 we see that the daughter-in-law of Eli, after hearing that the Philistines had taken the Ark, named her newborn son Ichabod because.she said that "The glory is departed from Israel because the Ark of God was taken..." The truth was the reverse of what she said- the glory and presence of God was departed therefore the Ark was taken. God's glory could not dwell with the people because of their sins and idol worship. Their focus was upon the symbol rather than God.

Like Gideon's ephod and the Ark of the Covenant, the symbols must not become more important than our focus on God. The focus was on the bread rather than on what Christ did for us on the cross. The bread itself became the issue and focus of communion. When I tried to explain that, the ones involved did not agree with my thinking. I shocked them when I told them that I have already taken communion in my own home using whatever juice I happened to have in the house and a Cheez-it cracker. I did that because I was facing a problem and I needed to remind myself and encourage myself that God has promised to answer and meet my needs, because Jesus died and became the "Mediator of a better covenant" (Heb. 8:6) I could claim every verse and promise in the Word.

Paul had problems with the Christians in Colossae who were caught up in tradition and Jewish legalism. These words apply to the Christian church today as well:

> "If then you have died with Christ to material ways of looking at things... and teachings of externalism why do you submit to rules and regulations? Referring to things all of which perish with being used." (Col. 2:20-22)

These kinds of issues show us that there is still a lot of legalism in the church and that is not a new problem. Even before the church was established and Jesus was on earth the religious leaders were legalistic. I saw a book one time on a sale table entitled *ThePharisees' Guide to Total Holiness.* I decided to buy it. I do not remember all I read, but I do remember the author pointed out that the Pharisees started out with good intentions. They wanted to teach the Jews how to be blameless before God and to do this they felt that had to further define the Ten Commandments. For each of the original ten they had inserted a dozen or more rules about how to obey each commandment. For example, one commandment states "Remember the Sabbath." The Pharisees felt it would help the people to explain how to do that, so they came up with all types of man's regulations. There was a set limit for a distance to walk. People should not spit on the ground for that would be watering, but if they spit on a stone it was fine. Women were not to look into their mirrors (actually metal not glass) because they might see an unwanted hair and pluck it and that would be reaping on the Sabbath. I wonder what churches would look like today if no one took a quick look at themselves in a mirror before getting to the service! The author went on to say that the Pharisees did this for the purpose of building a fence of safety for the people so they couldn't cross the line and break the law. Their intent was probably okay, but the detailed rules were not Biblical. We know that Jesus condemned the Pharisees for laying burdens on the people that they themselves could not keep. Jesus warned them that their traditions were actually replacing God's Word:

> "...in vain do they worship me, teaching for doctrines the commandments of men. For laying aside the commandment of God, ye hold the tradition of men...full well ye reject the commandment of God, that ye may keep your own tradition." (Mk. 7:7-9)

Another example of churches establishing traditions is the interpretation of I Timothy 2:9, "...that women adorn themselves in modest apparel..." That is a Biblical principle but what is modesty? If we are honest we will have to admit that what we might call modest today would have not been modest in the early 1900's. I have been at churches that create a long list of modest dress guidelines- sleeves must cover the elbows, shoes must be enclosed, no makeup, and the height of the collar and length of the dress are specified. In some churches even the style and colors of clothes are stipulated. Like the Pharisees, the intent is to make people holy, but that isn't holiness, especially when it causes strife and resentment. People conform but inside are rebelling. They are like the little boy whose mother made him sit in the corner for his poor behavior, but when asked by his dad what he was doing there, he responded by saying- Mommy made me sit in the corner, but I'm standing up inside.

We should not be against traditions just because they are traditions. Traditions can help us to be organized and to have stability. There is a peace and comfortableness in consistency and ritual, but we need to be sure we stay focused on the right things and understand what is tradition and what is Biblical. If we don't understand that, when something is done a little differently we can create strife, bitterness and even drive the unsaved from the church. We also need to be sure we do not offend baby Christians by enforcing man's rituals and rules that become bondage. God is not moved by ceremonial formalism or outward religious show.

Preserving traditions as a necessary part of our Biblical theology can turn into sour grapes. It is a sign of immaturity. Traditions can be nice if mixed with liberty. When I was living at home with my mom and I was teaching school, my mother always had only vanilla ice cream in the freezer. I once asked her if she knew they sold other flavors. She said she bought vanilla because she could combine it with many other things but we never did. When I lived in my own apartment I always had ice cream in my freezer. It was usually vanilla because it was traditional and you could combine it with many other things. I have changed since then. Now most of the time you will find only Black Cherry Grande in my freezer! Am I hung up on tradition? There is freedom in my tradition, because I know I am free to buy any flavor I want to and when I visit someone I will eat their favorite flavor and even enjoy it. My traditions should be like that. I like mine, but I can not only enjoy yours but won't criticize yours. There is a liberty for differences.

Some churches equate traditions with holiness. Here is a thought provoking quote from Rick Joyner found on his website: morningstarministries.org:

> True holiness is not legalism but love. The reason the bride wants to be without spot or wrinkle is not out of the fear that if she is not perfect her bridegroom will smite her, but because she is so in love with him that she wants to be perfect for him. This is the difference of being driven by legalism, which is fear based, and being motivated by the love that fulfills the law. That is why our primary goal should be to love more. The Lord affirmed that the most important commandments were to love God above all things and to love one another. If we love God, we will not worship idols. If we love others we will not steal, murder, or even envy them. The Lord replaced the "do nots" of the law with positives – love God and love one another because then we will fulfill all of the "do nots."

Then when the community and the unsaved look at us Christians and the church they will not see bitter grapes but will see love in action. They will not see bondage and meaningless traditions, but a place of joy, peace and love.

Some traditions may be good but there must be freedom. When the tradition becomes more important to me than other people, the result will be friction. Sometimes whole groups of Christians leave and cause a church split or the traditionalists will experience anger and frustration that leads to a root of bitterness.

We must not make a spiritual religious practice from choices. We must not try to find Scripture to support turning choices into Biblical directives by taking verses out of context. We must distinguish between traditions or personal preferences and Biblical charges.

Many older Christians ignore and dislike the new because it exposes their own weaknesses and emptiness. Either of these results will produce a crop of bitter grapes that will create a stench to the community and especially the unsaved.

Traditions and church practices are good in that they help create stability and order, but they must be understood as "choice" practices not Biblical commands. When these practices which are just that -practices- are questioned we need to examine them in light of Scripture. I must not become bitter over a method of doing a good thing. Some traditions are simply bitter and create bitterness and are not worth preserving. A branch on the vine always must dwell in truth but must be constantly growing and changing. We must not cause people to question the very character of Jesus, the Vine Himself. We must not let our own branches become fruitless.

Think about it

1. Can you name some of your church traditions that are Biblically based?

2. Can you think of some practices that are just traditions? Should they be preserved?

3. Do you have any church practices that would be a hindrance to a non-Christian or a new Christian? What should be done about it?

4. What church styles or methods are there that have changed in the last few years? Are they good or bad changes? Why?

Chapter 10

Branches Sometimes Produce Sour Fruit

One of the blessings of living in Zimbabwe, Africa is the climate. We rarely had frost and never had snow, but it was chilly on some winter mornings. I did miss the snow but the advantage was that it made it possible to have citrus trees in our yard. We had a grapefruit tree just outside the back door. It was a real joy to go out on a cold winter morning (cold for us was in the forties) and pick a fresh ripe grapefruit off the tree to eat for breakfast. We also had orange trees. When I settled back in the northeastern United States I found that I was not very happy with the citrus bought at the local markets. It took several years for me to get adjusted to fruit picked before fully ripe and shipped to our locale. I find it is harder to buy ripe fruit of almost any kind in our area because of the need to pick it a bit green so it has a longer shelf life. I have adjusted to eating most of the fruits when not fresh from the tree except for peaches. I still prefer going directly to the orchard and trying to get fresh and ripe fruit.

I also like grapes. Grapes were not real common for us in Zimbabwe. It is nice to enjoy them all year around in the States. When I go shopping I usually look at the grapes to see the price. On the whole it seems to me that grapes are expensive. When the price is right or when I just have a real craving for grapes I figure it is time to buy. When I do buy grapes I want them to be sweet and ripe. If I take home grapes and find they taste sour I am disappointed. I don't know much about what makes grapes sour but I think it must be for the same reason other fruit is sour- it was picked too soon, before it was ripe and shipped and kept in cold storage until ready to be put out in the market. As a result the fruit never gets fully ripe. It looks nice and can even feel soft, but it is not ripe and therefore sour and/or tasteless.

There are several references to sour grapes in the Bible. The Hebrew word used for sour grapes unripe or immature grapes that are sour. When I was a young child growing up, I would eagerly wait for the concord grapes to get ripe in September. I would check them every day for a few weeks, knowing the time was coming for ripe grapes. As soon as they looked purple I was sure they were ready and I would pick one. I'd pop it into my mouth, but if I was rushing the season, instead of a sweet juicy treat my lips would pucker up and that grape came out faster than it went in. They looked ripe but they were not yet quite sweet. They were immature grapes. I finally learned that in New York, where I grew up, we needed to wait for a little colder weather to ripen the grapes. Usually after the first frost the concord grapes were sweetest.

The Israelites had a proverb which we find in Scripture. "...The fathers have eaten sour grapes, and the children's teeth are on edge." (Ezek. 18:2) The Jews seemed to use this as an excuse for their idolatry. Much like some people today, they blamed their disobedience on their parents. They were saying in that proverb, that it wasn't their fault they sinned. It is true that we are affected by the generations which preceded us. There are generational curses, in spite of the fact that some Christians refuse to believe it. They will say sin comes from environment, but the environment that caused the parent to do certain sins actually comes from demonic influence. Somewhere in the ancestral lineage an individual allowed satan to invade his life and those same demons will continue to influence and tempt the following generations. Jesus broke that generational curse (or demonic powers) ability to control families.

In the account of the crucifixion we read that Jesus was offered "vinegar (wine) mingled with gall" but refused to drink but later he was offered sour vinegar and apparently drank it. Jesus drank the sour grapes to take away our generational curses as well as shedding His blood to take away our sins.

Just as we must ask for Jesus to forgive our sins and to make us righteous so we must ask Him to take away the generational curse-the sour grapes of our forefathers to be set free. Asking for these things from Jesus does not mean we will never sin again, but it breaks the power of sin and its strong hold on our lives. We need to keep reminding our flesh that it is dead and build our spirit. We do have the choice to break these curses and refuse to practice the same sins or to live under them.

In Ezekiel's day it was much harder for the Jews to break them because they had limited knowledge and did not have the Holy Spirit indwelling them continuously. Jesus had not yet come to redeem them from the curse of the law. Ezekiel was telling the Jews that a day was coming when that proverb would not be used because a Redeemer, Who would give power to break those curses was coming. However they still could not use this proverb against God's coming judgment. God did not excuse the sins of the Jews, particularly that of idolatry, just because their forefathers had practiced it. Each man was (and we still are) responsible for his own decisions and actions. Ezekiel clearly spoke the Word of God to the Jews who were making excuses:

> "The soul that sinneth it shall die. The son shall not bear the iniquity of the father, neither shall the father bear the iniquity of the son: the righteousness of the righteous shall be upon him, and the wickedness of the wicked shall be upon him." (Ezek. 18:20)

Today, just as in Ezekiel's day, we cannot excuse our actions by placing blame on our ancestors. The Old Testament Law was given so man could know what was right and what was sin and people had to make choices. They did not have the Holy Spirit indwelling them so the Law was given to help them to know how to act. The law that was given in Exodus 21:24- "Eye for eye, tooth for tooth, hand for hand, foot for foot" was not to demand retribution but to control or limit vengeance. It was to prevent rash unfair treatment for acts of violence or accidents. Nowadays we have a greater responsibility for our actions because we have a personal relationship with God if we are Christians. We have an inner heart change.

The Jews looked forward to a new day, even though they did not comprehend all that the Messiah would do. Jeremiah also makes reference to this coming day:

> "In those days they shall say no more, the fathers have eaten a sour grape, and the children's teeth are set on edge...Behold, the days come, saith the Lord, that I will make a new covenant with the house of Israel and the house of Judah." (Jer. 31:29, 31)

Jeremiah also tells them the day is coming when every man will die for his own iniquities and when an individual eats sour grapes his own teeth will be set on edge. We live in that day and we have no excuse for our actions. I have heard people make excuses for wrong behavior by saying- I can't help it. I'm just like my mother or just like my father. We may think that that is a legitimate excuse for sin, but it is eating sour grapes and it not only puts that person's teeth on edge, but it can leave a sour taste in the lives of others around him.

In Isaiah 18 we see another symbolic use of sour grapes. The prophet Isaiah under God's direction predicts judgment against Israel's enemies. In verse 5 God predicted this:

> "...When the bud is perfect, and the sour grape is ripening in the flower, he shall both cut off the sprigs...and cut down the branches."

In other words before this enemy (some think it was Ethiopia and others Assyria) can harvest Judah, i.e. take away her goods, God will deal with them as easily as the vine- dresser cuts down a vine. At this time God was still showing grace and mercy to the Jews, but the day was coming when their enemy would carry them away. He was still waiting to see a harvest of fruit from His chosen people.

Hosea does not mention sour grapes but he does say of Israel, "Their drink is sour." (Hos. 4:18) I thought about sour drink and asked God to show me why He used that metaphor. The Holy Spirit is referred to as wine. I believe God has sweet wine for His children. Sour wine is poor quality wine. Israel continually chose to worship idols instead of God. They were choosing a low life instead of serving the Living God. How tragic that the fruit they were producing was sour and the wine of their idols was also sour. Therefore they didn't realize or experience the blessed life.

Perhaps today we Christians produce sour grapes and drink sour wine because we, too, have idols in our lives. We need to understand when we put anything before God we live a life seeking pleasure in sour wine. We remain immature because we cannot grow up in God if we do not develop an intimate and vibrant daily relationship with Him. There are many things that are not sin in and of themselves but can become a hindrance to maturing and therefore sinful behavior. Perhaps we are more conscientious about reading the daily newspaper or watching the daily news than spending time in the Word and in communion with God.

Being physically busy seems easier for most of us than sitting quietly before the Lord. That is what it means to be sitting on the fourth chair described in chapter 4. I taught at a Christian school for a number of years and like so many Christian ministries the problem of limited finances was a major one. As faculty, staff and parents we spent many hours in fund raising ventures. It seemed like it was easier to get volunteers for that than to get them to promise to pray for the school. I had one parent admit that she found it easier to help make pies for eight hours than to volunteer to pray about the school's financial needs for an hour. I heard a preacher once say that God wants our worship more than our work. We might be amazed how much time and effort we could actually save if we were willing to spend more time communicating with God. That means listening as well as talking. This does not mean I do nothing but I set priorities in how I use my time.

A number of years ago the church I was attending was trying to devise a plan to increase attendance. I was on a committee that was to visit the members to ask what they thought we needed to do to grow. People had a variety of suggestions but I was amazed that not one suggested we get together to pray and seek God's plan for outreach.

Today any church can buy one of dozens of books on how to increase attendance. These writers have creative ideas and programs for outreach that worked at their churches, but God has His unique plan for every church to grow and it isn't a "one size fits all" program. Each church or congregation has its own unique community and only God knows how to best reach that area. However like volunteering to bake pies, most people find it easier to read a book and adopt another man's ideas than to spend time seeking God's direction. It is like drinking sour wine or producing sour grapes. Christians need to mature in their faith in God more than in another person's ideas.

Immature Christians have been a part of the church since its conception. Paul confronted this problem in the Corinthian church. He used the term "carnal." In I Corinthians 3 he speaks to carnal or baby Christians. Too many immature Christians in a church create "envying and strife, and divisions" (verse 3). He reminds them that the wisdom of this world is foolishness with God. I have seen that in churches. A common phrase that I think describes the world's foolishness and should not describe the church is being "politically correct." We need to be "Biblically correct." We live and practice the love walk of 1 Corinthians 13. We need to be kind and loving toward our brothers and sisters, as well as to the unsaved, but we cannot focus on being politically correct in order to be loved and accepted by the world by doing and saying what they do.

Last of all a sign of sour grapes being grown in a Christian's life is believers with lists of personal agendas for their church. We insist on having our own way and steer the church's services and programs in our direction whenever possible. We are often legalistic and do not like new things. We are those of the second generation Christians. We can trace our ancestry though the church membership records. Because we are so busy with our personal preferences, we do not have time for an intimate relationship with God and although we may have been a Christian for years and come from a strong Christian heritage, we can remain immature and don't know it. We justify ourselves by saying and thinking we are doing it for the good of the church and for the glory of God. The fruit produced is sour grapes of immaturity. Often there can be several groups vying with each other for control.

This causes arguing, fighting over worship styles, music, dress and buildings. All that energy could be put into ripening and maturing grapes, if we would change our focus to Christ and His Word.

We need to understand that sour grapes of man-made traditions will not bring people to the church or to Christ. We can spoil our outreach to the community by arguing over the man-made traditions. We have people in the church that have never grown up and although they want to grow and produce fruit in their lives they have been kept blinded by unimportant issues and personal preferences and programs for the church. We need to stay tuned to the Lord and learn to hear His voice for direction in our church.

Today the agriculturists are constantly working to produce more and better fruit- sweeter, bigger, juicier even more disease resistant. Yet sometimes we want to hold on to the older varieties. We feel they were better, and to us they might be. However that is simply a matter of personal taste.

As we get older it does get harder to make changes or even want to think about changes, but we need to understand that God is never in a rut. He is "new every morning" and always up to something new and we need to keep pace with Him. God wants to direct our lives to make people hungry for Him and not set their teeth on edge when they watch us.

Think about it

1. Do you know people or do you yourself have faults/sins that you excuse by blaming your parents of forefathers? How can we change that?

2. Do we live a mediocre life? What is the result of living that way?

3. Do I have any pet or personal agendas for my church? Do I feel others do? How can I deal with this individual?

Chapter 11

Even Branches and Grapes Have Enemies

Although most of us are aware that there are people who do not really like us, we probably really do not think of having enemies that would like to completely destroy us. I never happened to be in a place where some type of emotionally disturbed individual takes a gun and shoots randomly at people he doesn't even necessarily know. I have never been involved in a military battle so I suppose I have been protected most of my life. However I did have one experience that made me realize I was hated and could have been killed. It was when I was a missionary in Zimbabwe, Africa.

Zimbabwe has a history of British colonization. Let me give you a simplified history lesson about Zimbabwe which was formerly called Rhodesia. Under the British statesman Cecil Rhodes, the Matabele people who lived in the area of what is now Zimbabwe were forced to surrender their land and the territory was named Rhodesia. Under white rule Rhodesia declared its independence from Britain in 1965 in order to maintain its white control. While I was living and teaching in Rhodesia in 1969, the white government created a new constitution that was approved by the majority of voters (whites) to prevent the black African majority from ever gaining control of the government. In the 1970's fighting broke out between the government soldiers and black African guerrillas.

I was living and teaching high school at a mission school for black Africans during those years. We heard from time to time about guerrilla attacks upon whites who owned large farms or businesses and even a few mission stations had experienced problems. We felt relatively safe because we were training young blacks and not supporting the white government. We did not realize the deep hatred for white people, which was understandable, but we were not aware that this hatred included the missionaries. I always felt that the blacks knew that we were in Africa to help them and that we did not treat them or see them as the majority of White Europeans who lived there saw them. The whites did not understand the missionaries because they did see we were different.

One evening just as we were getting ready for bed we heard shooting of an automatic rifle outside our house. We were being attacked by a band of guerrilla soldiers. It was a very frightening experience, but miraculously no one was killed. It was the first time I had ever really felt I had an enemy - one that did not mind killing me just because I was white. One who really was indirectly attacking a white government that he hated.

This is an excellent parallel to the Christian's life. We have an enemy who hates us just because we are a Christian. He attacks us as an indirect strike against a God that he hates. His name is satan. He is our enemy. He will try various ways to attack us. He tries to get us to fail in our lives so that he can point his finger at us and accuse us before God. satan is called the "accuser of the brethren" in Revelation 12:10. It is like accusing a child before a parent by telling the parents of the child's weaknesses and failures. To make us fail and disobey God is satan's desire and he will attack us in the three areas of our life- body, soul or spirit. One of the ways he does that is to get us to take our eyes off him and to get involved and focused on the problems. Paul tells us in Ephesians 6 that we need to take the shield of faith to quench the fiery darts of the wicked. The word refers to the devil but also carries the idea of evil influences. We as Christians have an enemy who will not only attack us directly but also through demons and situations and people around us.

In Paul's days the soldiers often did actually shoot fiery darts at their enemies. The strategy was to set fire to the grass and wood roofs so that the enemy had to take their focus off the battle and turn away to put out the fires, thus making them vulnerable for attack.

That is what satan likes to do to us Christians to get our attention diverted from him and look at God, other people (even Christians), and situations to blame for our problems.

We have spiritual enemies just as the grapevines and grapes have natural enemies. Solomon in the Song of Solomon warns us of these temptations and sin will attack by illustrating it through grapevines. He tells us that we need to take care of the little foxes that spoil the grapes. Apparently in Bible times in Israel there were foxes or some believe they were a type of jackal that got into the vineyards and spoiled the vines. Although we think of foxes and jackals as meat eaters, some varieties do eat bulbs and fruit. Whatever the animal, we know from the context of Song of Solomon that little foxes spoiled the vineyards.

In vineyards today beetles will attack the leaves of the grapevines. In my area of Pennsylvania we have the Japanese beetle that will come in summer and eat the leaves of the grapevines but not many other insects or diseases attack grapes. In other regions of the United States and in Europe a plant lice phylloxera can be a problem. It feeds on the leaves and roots of the plant by sucking out all the sap, causing the fruit, leaves and vines to eventually die. Grape growers need to be alert to prevent the destruction of their crops.

In the Song of Solomon chapter 2, Solomon mentioned "the little foxes that spoil the grapes." He was referring to the little things that we might not notice or try to drive away, but that will in time destroy us. It is often the little things that defeat us in our Christian walk. We can make excuses and say that a thing is not specifically mentioned as sin, so what is the harm? There are a number of small "things" that can spoil our fruit.

We need to learn to listen to God and obey Him, because even other Christians, meaning to instruct us in God's will can give wrong advice. When I returned from Zimbabwe I was interested in teaching at a particular Christian School. When I told one of the teachers who had lived with me in Zimbabwe and was teaching there, she told me it was not right for me to apply for a job at Shalom. There was an older missionary lady who had applied for the same job and I should let her have it, out of respect for her and because I was younger she felt I could get a job in many other places. I listened to her and declined the job. I realize now that that was human advice, not God's leading. I did find another job teaching in another place for a year but halfway through that year the older lady who was at Shalom met a widower and they planned to get married but she had to wait until the end of the year. God had a plan for each of us and I was to teach at Shalom that year but I got my focus on people instead of God. God had grace and gave me another job for the year, but I never really felt comfortable in it. It was God's second best. The following summer I did apply again at Shalom and got the position. I started teaching there in the fall replacing the teacher who was by then was happily married. This was not a serious lifetime sidetrack. But it was the one year in my teaching career in which I found limited joy. It was uncomfortable to realize I was not in God's perfect plan. God worked with all of us through this, but it is an illustration of missing God's best by letting satan use people to make us miss God's plan. He will use any situation or person to try to make us miss God's best.

In our Christian life we must be aware of our enemies. satan will lead us into sin or just cause us to miss God's best if he can. We need to be able to recognize the source of attack. We need to know our enemy. satan is the source of all sin directly or indirectly. He will attack directly or use other people, situations or our own sinful nature to gain victory over us. The teacher who told me not to take the job from another lady was a godly woman and meant well. She was trying to help another Christian but we need to learn to hear from God. When someone tells us what God wants for us we need to cover that with prayer and be sure it is God's leading.

satan is a very clever strategist, but he is limited. He has used the same tactics against people through the ages. We can learn his plan of attack by looking at a very familiar parable recorded in three of the four Gospels. In Mark 4 Jesus told His disciples that if they did not understand this parable, they could not understand the other parables. In Mark 4:13 He said, "...Know ye not this parable? And how then will ye know all parables?" This parable of the Sower and the Seed teaches us how satan works against us. He attacks the body first and sad to say often succeeds in destroying Christians and needs to go no further. If satan can't defeat us at the body or flesh level, he attacks the soul and then eventually our spirits. At any of these levels the temptation can come in the form of a very small one that we might not recognize as sinful.

In order to understand satan's attack, we must first clarify what is meant by body, soul and spirit. It is easy to define or grasp what is meant by our human bodies. It is the visible part of my existence that everyone can see. It includes my physical appetites and needs. The soul, although very closely intertwined with the body, is the mind, will and emotions. The third part of man is his spirit and it can also be difficult to separate from the soul. Because we are one man with three parts we can become confused as to which is which. For example hunger is a physical drive, but can also become a soul or emotional drive. The writer of Hebrews tells us that only the Word of God is able to help us to discern the difference:

> "For the word of God is quick, and powerful, and sharper than any two-edged sword, piercing even to the dividing asunder of soul and spiritually, and of the joints and marrow..." (Heb. 4:12)

As we read the parable in Mark 4 we find that after the word is sown the attacks of satan hit us. First in verse 17- "...affliction and persecution..." These are physical attacks against us from people trying to convince us that we should not be so "religious" or it can be physical diseases and ailments that make us question God and turn from Him. There have been some people who came to Christ and were fervent for Him and they came down with some disease that made them blame God and turn from Him. Sometimes it is a tragic accident or death that makes them bitter toward God. In many foreign countries there is actually physical persecution for the person who accepts Christ. These are satan's attack on the body. He will destroy the Word or Seed before it builds enough faith to resist satan.

If he cannot defeat us in that area, he will attack our soul- Verse 19- "cares of this world." These are brought against our emotions, mind and will. The cares that come might be worry, money issues, possessions, or family problems. Sometimes it is just being made fun of for being a Christian. In high school I had a friend that was not a Christian. She went along with a group of us to a Christian youth meeting. There she accepted the Lord and determined to follow Jesus, but when she got back to school on Monday her former friends quickly convinced her she had done the wrong thing. Every so often she would go along with us to a youth meeting and go forward to repent and rededicate herself to the Lord, but when she went back to school her non-Christian friends would tease her and advise her against being a fanatic and she would go back to her old lifestyle. She cared more about pleasing her friends than pleasing God. satan destroyed the Seed or Word before it could grow strong within her to realize that following Jesus was the better way.

Last of all if satan cannot cause the Word (Seed) to dry up within us before it produces fruit, he will attack our spirits which Mark 4:19 calls "lust of other things." This is a bit harder to understand because the spirit of man is the least definable part of us. It is our deep personality and sense of being. It is the real or true me.

To help understand this concept of satan's attack we can look at another portion of Scripture in I John 2:15, 16. John is warning Christians against loving the world and then explains the three areas that constitute man-body, soul, and spirit. He states what the world offers- "...the lust of the flesh, and the lust of the eyes, and the pride of life..." The lust of the flesh consists of things that appeal to the body- meeting the physical drives and appetites improperly. The lust of the eyes refers to things we possess and strive to possess. Things that bring us pleasure above God- appealing to the mind and emotions The pride of life is spirit related which is an incorrect self-image and concept of who we are without God or God priorities. It is really a type of self worship.

This plan of attack through these channels is as old as creation itself. It is the way satan attacked Eve and brought about the fall of the human race. In Genesis 3 we see that satan created a question in Eve's mind regarding the tree of good and evil. First she saw that the tree was "good for food"- the body's need. Next it was "pleasant to the eye"-emotionally gratifying. Thirdly it would "make one wise"- to spiritually become "...as gods knowing good and evil."

If we study a number of accounts from Scripture we will see a similar pattern of satan's actions directly upon us or by using other people. Last of all we will look at the temptations of Jesus. In Matthew 4 we find that Christ was faced with the same three basic temptations used by satan. It is necessary to remind you here that these three parts of man were created by God for good. When we use all our being in the way God meant for us, it is pleasing to God. But sin causes us to misuse and pervert them. In each phase of attack satan attempted the very Son of God to misuse His powers for personal gratification. Jesus was hungry after 40 days of fasting and satan tempted Him to use His miracle powers to meet His need. It was more than a temporary or at that moment thing. It was a temptation for Jesus to consider how He was going to spend His life of limitless authority and power. Would it be to just meet His personal physical needs? He was human and we know He got hungry and tired just as we do. Jesus was tempted with making bread for his body need. The second attack was for Jesus to use His powers to make a name for Himself by performing miracles that would be more like stunts of entertainment and bring world fame and praise. The last temptation was upon His spirit. Who would Jesus actually worship and serve? satan had gained the ownership of the world and its systems after Adam and Eve had surrendered their dominion on earth by eating from the forbidden tree. satan was offering Jesus world power if He would just bow down and worship him. Jesus did not give in to any misuse of His body, soul or spirit. He experienced the victory of the overcoming life.

We Christians have enemies that can slowly "suck the life" from us. Often it is so gradual that we don't realize it until we are living a defeated life and filled with the sense of hopelessness in even trying to obey God. We might be living under extreme guilt. satan delights in making us feel guilty to keep us from seeking God. I remember a student of mine in a Christian school where I was teaching. I noticed that her usually happy countenance had gradually changed. When I asked her what was wrong she shared that God was dealing with a small issue in her life and she was struggling to obey. The issue was not even based on Scripture but rather related to traditions. However she was experiencing guilt over it, so she stopped reading her Bible and stopped praying. That made her feel more guilty and she pulled further away from God. satan was causing her to break her fellowship with God and stealing her peace and joy all over a tradition.

This can happen also when we choose to do the wrong thing and sin. satan tells us we are too bad to go to God and that keeps us from asking forgiveness and staying in fellowship. He will try to convince us that God no longer loves or even likes us. Perhaps he enjoys doing this to us even more when it is about keeping or breaking traditions. It becomes a vicious cycle, especially if we have bad habits with which we struggle. I recall reading about a man who was guilty of exaggeration (a kind way to say speaking untruthfully.) After he became a Christian he tried to stop doing that. One day almost before he had time to think he did it. When he prayed that night he remembered the sin and asked God to forgive Him. He said, "I did it again." He heard God say, "Did what again?"

"I spoke a lie by exaggerating," he answered.

"Oh, did you do that before?" God responded. "You're forgiven." Isn't it wonderful that God not only forgives, but forgets when we repent? We can come to Him and be set free from these little "foxes", so we must not let satan bring guilt that makes us hide from God. Let God speak conviction that brings us to repentance.

satan is clever but we do not need to fear him for he is not creative. He uses the same plan and methods over and over. He attacks us first on the flesh level. We can so easily be caught there but we know if we overcome the flesh he will attack our soul which is our mind, will and emotions. It is probably rare that he will need to attack the spirit for all too often he has defeated us on the first or second level. We need to be aware of these levels so we are prepared to meet him with Scripture and Godly wisdom. It takes us humans time to learn and grow, but we can learn how to defend ourselves and produce a fruitful life so that we do not misuse our basic talents and gifts. We can learn to be victorious but it isn't an overnight program.

There are enemies we need to face. satan will use a set variety of methods. He attacks us in our body, soul (will and emotions) and even our spirit. By understanding this and seeing how Jesus defeated satan, we can more easily detect the source and can use the right strategy to be victorious. We are reminded again of John's words in I John 4:4- "... greater is he that is in you, than he that is in the world." If satan uses our own weaknesses or an enemy or even best friends we can keep our focus on God and seek His face to know truth.

God has made the necessary provisions to protect the branches of the Vine so that they will not live in defeat but be fruitful. The way to protect ourselves is to stay intimately connected to the Vine.

Think about it

1. How can little things that may even be good become sin? How do they become sin?

2. Have you ever received advice from a Christian friend that you felt was wrong or turned out to be wrong for you? How did you handle it?

3. What are some temptations for our body (physical)? Soul (mind, emotions)? Or our spirit? Do these areas of temptations intertwine?

4. What is the difference between guilt and conviction?

Chapter 12

No Fruit at All

While I was teaching in Africa, sometimes during a school break, I would go visit a nurse friend of mine at another mission station. She enjoyed showing me around the hospital and talking about some of the patients there. One time while I was there a local African evangelist went home to be with the Lord and I had the opportunity (?) of helping her dress the corpse for the funeral. Zimbabwe does not follow a rigid time schedule, and has limited means of travel, especially in the rural areas. We had to wait until the family brought in this man's best suit for the funeral. There mode of travel was by foot. We do not embalm the bodies, so by the time the family came back with the suit rigor mortise had already started. We did finally manage to get the body dressed for the funeral. Physical death is sad. It is natural to miss a loved one, but we can say with the Apostle Paul-"To die is gain," and we can find comfort in knowing we will meet again.

There was another man who was in the hospital who had been there for years- just lying in a bed. There was nothing physically wrong with him. He had been checked and tested by doctors but this man insisted he was sick and dying and refused to get out of bed. After a number of years his muscles and body atrophied and he actually could no longer get out of bed. What a tragedy it was so see how one can eventually become completely useless when he could have chosen to be up and about enjoying life for those years.

It makes me wonder if there is something like spiritual rigor mortise or spiritual atrophy. Is it possible these types of conditions can be experienced by a Christian? Can this happen to us spiritually? Can we get "stiff" from not moving or doing anything? God called the Children of Israel **stiff necked** or obstinate a half dozen times during their wandering in the wilderness. Moses told Israel that God didn't give them the land because they were righteous but because of His promise to their forefathers:

> "Not for thy righteousness or for the uprightness of thine heart, dost thou go to possess their land....that He may perform the word which the Lord sware unto thy fathers..." (Deut. 9:5)

In Acts we read that Stephen when disputing with a group of Jews told them that they were stiff necked and "do always resist the Holy Ghost. "They were like the dead man or the man who just decided he didn't want to move and became stiff from lack of exercise. Is it possible for us to accept Christ as our personal Savior and live for years and never produce any fruit at all? Can we be spiritually dead or become spiritually atrophied? We can attend church regularly and keep all the church rules and even believe in all the right doctrines. We can enjoy singing the hymns and choruses and even support the church financially and never produce fruit. Do we become obstinate in our practices and traditions? We are content to be involved in the church program so everybody thinks we are doing fine, but personally we are indifferent to moving into a deeper walk with God and exercising our God given purpose in life. (Another fourth chair example)

Israel was guilty of becoming spiritually atrophied and therefore producing no fruit, even though they followed the rituals of Judaism. In Hosea 10:1 God said, "Israel is an empty vine, he bringeth forth fruit unto himself."

After Israel entered the Promised Land some of the tribes had become content to stay where they were. In Joshua 18 we find that seven of the tribes that had entered the Promised Land had not yet divided their land into its proper apportionment. Joshua asked them why they hadn't and then sent three men from each of these tribes to scout out the land that was to be allotted. Why had these people not moved forward into their promised section?

Later in the book of Judges we discover they still had not finished the task God had given them. They did not drive out the enemies. We read the phrase "did not drive out" as an accusation against a number of the tribes of Israel. Were they content to stay where they were and enjoy a limited victory? Was it laziness that kept them from going forward? Had they lost their vision and dreams of the abundant life God had promised or was it their lack of faith? We are not told why, but they atrophied.

Are we that way today? Do we get saved and just live in that experience. Do we enjoy being babies and not want to grow up? It might be called a "Peter Pan" complex! We lack the drive and persistence to keep growing and maturing. We keep everything just as it is. However we do not produce grapes. Perhaps we are like the fig tree that Jesus cursed because it had no fruit- just leaves. Is there a fear factor in growing up? Are we afraid of the enemy and do not trust God enough to bring us the victory?

I really like asparagus. My sister really liked it too. We had a small patch of it where I grew up, but there never seemed to be enough at one time to get a very big helping, much less to have seconds. For some reason asparagus is expensive to buy, so I decided after a few years of living in our own home that I would start an asparagus patch- a large patch! I learned that it takes several years of growing before I could actually harvest asparagus. I also learned later that as new stalks come up you need to let them get thick and not pick the thin spindly stalks It takes time to mature but it does happen if you take good care of it. Later I learned that in order to keep weeds down you sprinkle salt on the patch. Salt does not harm or hinder the asparagus but it kills the weeds. Now I have not only all the asparagus I want, but enjoy sharing it with others. The goal in raising asparagus is to get plenty of "fruit" (I know it's a vegetable) and to be able to share. The same thing is true in our Christian lives. Why do we not want to mature and produce fruit? We can experience the joy of sharing with others. Perhaps fear of the unknown is holding us back. Maybe a lack of faith hinders our maturing. It might be that we do not grow because we are not sure what He might ask of us or fear He may fail us or we fail Him. Perhaps God will move in some unusual or new way and move us out of our comfort zone. I have seen fear stop the moving of God in a life as well as in a meeting.

One Sunday I was in a church service at a church where I was very involved. We had hired a new head pastor and I was sure he was not open to the moving of the Holy Spirit and the operation of the gifts. I was enjoying the worship being led by a visiting team. God was there. As we concluded our singing one member of the worship team told us he had a word from the Lord. There was an individual in that service that needed an emotional healing. As he was about to ask her to come forward, the head pastor took over the service by dismissing the team from the platform. When we questioned the pastor a few weeks later about his cutting off this word, he told us it was not of the Lord. I was sure it was just a matter of not wanting gifts of the Spirit free to work in the service, because I believed it was of the Lord. God had used this worship team in the use of the gifts at other times. Later I learned the pastor had missed God's direction in the service because he didn't allow the word to be finished. One of our other pastors said that a woman had called in the following Monday morning and said she was the one described in that word and wondered if the man who gave it could help her. I am not sure what happened to this lady but she missed getting help because the head pastor feared the gifts being used in his church. How it must grieve the Holy Spirit and the Father when He is cut off. When we cut off the Holy Spirit it is like pulling the buds off the grapevine and destroying the producing of grapes.

At my house I had two different grapevines on opposite sides of a trellis. The one produced delicious concord grapes and still does. The other never produced fruit. It grew leaves but no fruit. It never really developed or matured enough to produce fruit. Like the parable of the fig tree after three or four years I decided to "...cut it down, why cumbereth it the ground?" (Lk. 13:7) God is patient and waits for us to grow but we need to show persistence and perseverance. Recently I saw a quote on a church sign, "Lord, give me the persistence of a weed." That needs to be a prayer for all of us if we want to grow. Growing of fruit and the abundant life takes effort and persistence.

In Second Chronicles 24, we observe a similar attitude of indifference that was eventually overcome by one man's persistence.

Joash became King of Judah and determined to repair the temple. He gathered the Levites and priests and told them to collect money from the people to repair the Lord's house. He said, "...see that ye hasten the matter. Howbeit the Levites hastened it not." Again we might ask why they did not hurry, but we are not told. Perhaps they did not want to ask the people for money. Maybe they were afraid of the reactions of people to such a request. Asking people to give to the church even today can be difficult. Maybe they just didn't get around to it. We can conclude they didn't see it as something important. It was not top priority in their thinking. Are we Christians any different today? Are we lacking perseverance or do we ignore and deny the gifts of the Spirit? Are we are content just to be saved? Perhaps we do not know our authority and potential in God. We are described in II Timothy 3:5 - "Having a form of godliness, but denying the power thereof..." We do not practice the gifts and do not see signs and wonders in our churches or our lives. Many do not even believe they are available to us today, but believe they have passed away. Apathy, ignorance and indifference will not produce grapes, or rebuild temples.

There are also individual Christians and churches that do not produce fruit because of a "country club" mindset. We have a beautiful and well-kept church building and a congregation of respectable community people. We attend and support the church events and activities as long as they are of high quality and will gain the admiration (and even envy) of everyone in the neighborhood. We dress in our suits and ties and best dresses and expect everyone else to do the same. We invite the finest musicians to "perform" in our services and present only high standard programs. We hire only polished educated leaders and put creative members in charge of every phase of church life. We get to the place where we no longer know God's will for the church but we choose by professional and worldly standards. We do not want to invite visitors who don't look like they "fit in." We are fearful of having undignified sinners come into the services- the homosexuals, unmarried pregnant girls, people living together without proper and acceptable marriage ceremony. We will support city missions and overseas missionaries financially and with prayer, but we do not want to be involved with those of a lower class because these people might influence our young people. They take away the dignity of our appearance to the important community people. We even generously support the Salvation Army, crisis pregnancy ministries, and local city missions but do not want the people reached through these ministries to come to our church because they do not meet our standard or criteria as future members.

We have trouble with the song that says- "Come as you are to worship" because we feel we need to be good enough to come to God. We need to look right and not be offensive to God. The writer of Hebrews tells us to come boldly to the throne of God. God does not make any suggestions or a list of requirements for us to meet Him. All He wants is a reverent, contrite and humble heart. He will accept sincere worship and respond to our coming. God is not looking for perfection in the outward man, but for a perfect heart. We need to be sure we do not focus on the outward but see the hearts and needs of people who come to God.

When we are country club Christians, we are busy with the outward appearance and focus on that more than on developing an intimate relationship with God. I was told once that there was a lady in the church who wrote down what she wore each Sunday so she wouldn't wear the same outfit too often. We need to remember that God doesn't look at the outside. He doesn't notice if we are wearing a tie or shoes. He isn't concerned about whether we coordinate the colors of our outfits. He looks at the heart. That is why we can talk to Him freely even while taking a shower or bath!

At some churches the bulletin is very closely followed so there will be no interruptions or impromptu changes. Everything is so perfectly planned and timed that God isn't even a part of the program. I'm reminded of the man who got saved out of a derelict life in the gutter and went into a church to hear more about God. When he entered the building, he was met by several ushers who "ushered" him back out to the street. He walked away apologizing to the Lord for not getting into a church and the Lord said to him- "That is okay. I've been trying to get into that church for years!"

Many of us are afraid of the gifts being manifest because we would lose control of the service. Can't we trust God to do His will in His time? I am not saying we should not have a plan for our service but we need to allow God to change it when He wants to do something special for us. Perhaps the basic problem is that we do not have a desperate need for God.

One time I was invited to speak to a small home group of Christians. I talked about God meeting our every need- spiritually, financially and physically. At the end of the meeting one young fellow came up to me and said that it was all very interesting but he had no needs. He was getting along fine because he was a Christian and he had a secure high position in a growing business and he and his family were all healthy. So what I had said really had no practical place in his life. This is a country club attitude. It was the attitude of the Pharisees and religious leaders in Jesus' day. In Luke 18 Jesus talked about the Pharisee that came to God and thanked Him that he was just fine and reminded God that he was doing his religious duties. He was not like the Publican. He had it all together. That was the country club "church" of Jesus' day. We still have the same attitude in some churches today. Solomon said, "He that trusteth in his own heart is a fool; but whoso walketh wisely he shall be delivered."

In a country club church we have our focus on outward appearances not heart attitude. We do not see ourselves as fruitless branches because we are respectable. We can live on past experiences and blessings. We are content to build a respectable praiseworthy community Christian country club church. Putting appearances and past experiences above God's plan is a type of idol worship. We lose our zeal to grow and are content where we are. We have almost lost contact with the Vine, but we try to look like we are a healthy productive branch. But where is the fruit?

In the first chapter of Joel we find a mournful lament about Israel's spiritual condition. Is it the same for churches today whose programs and buildings are more important than obedience to God? Has God withdrawn His anointing from some of our churches? God says this through Joel:

> "He hath laid my vine waste...and cast it away...the new wine is
> dried up...be ye ashamed...O ye vinedressers...the vine is dried
> up...joy is withered away." (Joel 1:7-12)

Although we should always want to be our best for God, and enjoy the blessings of a beautiful church building, good music etc., we need to be sure these things do not take priority over God's plan or the needs of the community. These things should be the means to the end not an end in themselves. There needs to be one major goal for us and that is to cling to the Vine and keeping a close obedient intimate relationship with God.

Think about it

1. What are the characteristics of a fruitful life?

2. What is your God given vision or dream? Have you lost it? How can you revive it or feed it?

3. What is your top priority? What are your secondary priorities?

Chapter 13

No Microwave Fruit

Sometimes when I pray and ask God to help me I have a problem waiting for the answer. A number of years ago when I was teaching at Shalom Christian Academy I was living in an upstairs apartment that was rented to me by a family that knew I was on a small paycheck and they charged me a very low rent. I would spend September to June there and the summer up in New York State with my mother who lived alone. In the spring of 1982 my mother died and I planned to go up to the house that summer and help prepare it for sale. Before I left to go up to New York and do that my landlord told me he was planning to sell the house and my rent would double when I returned in the fall. It was more than I could afford on my salary so I began looking for a cheaper place to rent. When it was time for me to go up home for the summer I had no leads for a place to live. The family was kind enough to let me leave my limited belongings in the furnished apartment. I had been praying and felt frustrated because I had seen no answer to my prayers for a place to live in the fall and now I was going to be over 300 miles away from the area where I needed to find an apartment. I went up to my mother's house and started cleaning, sorting what we children wanted to keep and what we needed to sell. We set a date for sale in the middle of August so I planned to stay there until the end of August. At that point I had no idea where I would be or what I might need. I didn't know if I would be living in a furnished apartment or would have to furnish it. I didn't have a clue as to what I should keep from my mother's things. How many things did I need? My other two sisters had homes of their own so did not want or need large items. Should I keep a bedroom suite or the dining room furniture? What about the refrigerator and the washer and dryer? I had been praying all summer without seeing an answer to my questions. I prayed that God would somehow provide a place before the sale, so I could keep what I needed.

A few days before sale the phone rang and it was the mother of a fellow teacher and she told me how a neighbor had come to her and asked if she knew any teacher from Shalom that needed a place to live. They had a part of a house that her son and wife had just moved into. They had been recently married and were planning to farm, but the farmhouse was bigger than they wanted at that point and they hoped to rent out a section to a single person. I knew it was an answer to my prayer and without looking at it I said I would take it. I just had a deep peace that it was of God.

The rent was within my budget and it was a rural setting. They wanted to rent to a Christian and a single without children because of not wanting children to be around farm animals and equipment that would be dangerous for youngsters.

God did answer my prayer in a miraculous way even though I would have been pleased if it had happened months before. However I believe that God was teaching me a lesson about trusting Him and leaving the answer to His timing. That is not easy for us Americans today who have a "right away" mentality.

Our society today has a "minute rice" mentality. We want everything done right away- fast food restaurants, drive up windows, microwave meals and easy snacks, and instant oatmeal. However you can't produce fruit or make it ripen faster by putting it in the microwave. In today's world we seem to always be in a hurry. People don't have time to stop or yield at traffic signs. We dash through the yellow lights when they are really red. We have overnight deliveries and one hour or less photo prints. We have drive thru windows for everything from banking to prescriptions. Today we can contact people almost anywhere around the world in a matter of seconds, hearing their voices and actually seeing them.

When I was in Zimbabwe in the 60's and 70's our only contact with family and friends was by mail and that took over a week. We thought that was great. Sometimes, however, I would write home and ask a question and by the time my letter arrived in the States and the answer came back to me I had forgotten what I asked. Today missionaries around the world can make direct and often visual contact with people thousands of miles away.

Modern technology is a blessing and wonderful in many ways. Even our educational systems and institutions are constantly striving to teach children to read at an earlier age. All this has given us a mindset of speed that can be detrimental at times. Some things can't be rushed. They need time to mature. A perfect example is fruit, including grapes.

There are no microwave grapevines or grapes. Grapevines are started from growths called canes and the cuttings from these canes are stored until early spring. They are kept in a greenhouse/nursery for a year before being put out in the vineyard. The vines still do not produce a full crop for several years. You cannot hurry the process by putting the canes into a microwave. It takes time. In our "microwave" society we seem to have lost our patience for normal and natural processes and growth.

There are no instantly mature Christians. As with grapevines and grapes we must allow time for growth and fruit. We can instantly become a Christian by simply asking Christ to come into our hearts and lives, but that is the planting of the Seed or Word. Growth comes after that and takes time. With grapevines the amount and quality depends on how well the vine is tended and nourished. The same is true for Christians. If we want good fruit we must put care in nourishment and fruit which comes from the Vine. Even after some growth, pruning is necessary to produce good fruit. There are no shortcuts for producing fruit. That is why it is not wise to place a new Christian in a prominent position. Sometimes this happens when a famous athlete, celebrity or public figure accepts Christ as Savior. We need to be sure they are starting to grow. Also we need to remember that we cannot expect new baby Christians to conform to the ideal Christian lifestyle immediately.

Growth of any sort takes time- naturally and spiritually. If you prune a grape vine too harshly or too soon it may shrivel and die. The same thing is true for new and young Christians. If we expect too much too soon from them, pointing out all the areas in which **we** want to see change, they may never mature but will die, because it seems too difficult. On the other hand we need to encourage growth and pray for them. If we notice some particular issue/habit or behavior that we know is sinful we need to pray for them and let God clearly direct us before speaking to them. God has a plan to mature them and He may use us or find another way to show them truth and conviction. The amount of time for maturing will vary for different individuals. Let God do His work in His time and manner.

I know of a church where a man and his family came for a Sunday service and accepted the Lord. The church was happy about that but concerned because he owned a local tavern and during the week he served liquor to people. Some folks approached the pastor and insisted that this man had to be confronted, but the pastor wisely responded by telling them to pray and let God do the "pruning." After a short time the man closed his business because he realized that God was not pleased with his owning and running that type of business. As a result this family was not offended or embarrassed. God did the pruning.

A similar thing happened in my family. My oldest sister became a Christian a few years ago. I was happy about that, but it bothered me that she continued to use God's name for emphasis when talking. I debated talking to her about it, but God told me to keep quiet. We were visiting my original home church and the former pastor, who was in a new church plant, told a story of how a lady in his community became a Christian and God corrected her for using His name as slang. On our way home, my sister asked if she ever did that. I told her as kindly as I could that I thought she did sometimes. She had not realized she did, but stopped doing it. I was thankful that God took care of it without **my** help! Growth takes time. There is no instant fruitfulness. We need to encourage the new believers and some older ones that are still struggling to mature to spend time with God and learn to hear Him speak. We must not play Holy Spirit (and we never are to step in His place). When tempted to force maturity on others we need to look at ourselves and see that we are still growing. Our grapes might be a bit more developed, but there is always room for more. You can no more rush maturity on people than you could force a piece of fruit to come out of the blossom by pulling it apart.

One time I was frustrated with a Christian whom I felt had acted sinfully. That evening while on my bed I thought about that individual and told God that I, even though I really knew it was not a Christian's love response, suggested to God that I thought it would be a good idea if God "smacked" him. Immediately I heard God telling me that if He were in the smacking business when His children acted improperly, I might be the first one in line! How amazing God's love, mercy and patience are. I am well aware that I need time to mature so I can't expect instant fruit in someone else.

Although we see that maturing takes time, it is necessary for us to learn the things we need to do in order to grow. God is faithful to speak to us and show us how, but we need to realize we have a responsibility for growth as well. We cannot be like the woman who prayed these words- "Lord, give me patience and I want it **right** now."

As we work with God and understand it takes time we will be able to enjoy growing in our Christian lives and can encourage and enjoy other branches on the Vine as they become more like Jesus.

Think about it

1. What are characteristics of a mature Christian?

2. What do I find most annoying about other Christians that make me think they are immature? Does that reveal something to me about myself?

3. How can I become more mature in my own life?

4. How can I help others to mature?

Chapter 14

Creating a Fruitful Vineyard

While teaching in Africa I was privileged to teach Bible to the African young people. The educational system was still under British rules and one of the required courses was Bible. All the students took Bible and along with their other subjects they had to take government written tests at the end of each year. It was nice because although they were tested on facts, one could teach practical life lessons through the year. I tried to make it applicable to their lives.

When I returned to the States I had the opportunity of teaching at Christian schools and was given Bible to teach to tenth graders and again I enjoyed it. At that time I was actually teaching ethics and although based on Bible facts and principles it was a very practical course for everyday living. I was so thankful that I had had a lot of Bible courses when at Messiah College although it had come about by human error. I believe it was directed by God for He knew how much I needed that background.

When I started my third year of college the regular registrar who had been planning my courses was on sabbatical leave and his substitute Mr. Heisey talked to me at the beginning of the year. He was concerned because he had heard I was thinking about doing missions work and he felt I had very little Bible background for that, so he changed my course and that year I had a wonderful assortment of Old and New Testament book studies. When Mr Heisey suggested that I take a year of Systematic Theology, I was a bit hesitant. The name itself sounded boring. The class was made up of a group of male students interested in the ministry and a few pastors who came to get more Bible training or degrees to aid their careers. As it turned out this was about the best course I ever took. There was one other lady in class so we took it upon ourselves to try to keep up with or even surpass these men who actually knew a lot more than we did. We ladies really studied hard so were able to keep our grades equal to or some times better than the men. It was frustrating to some of them. When it came to discussing and arguing issues we had very little to say, but we knew a secret that the men didn't know about are teacher. We knew what he wanted on his tests and so knew how to study for tests. We noticed that his exams were always essay questions and very general, for example- Explain the Trinity. Now that is quite a question. Whole books have been written by Bible scholars trying to explain that. We took very complete notes during his lectures and wrote everything we could on the test paper using his notes. The fellows knew more than we did so felt they didn't have to study for tests and wrote just a little. We were always the last ones to leave the room on test days. The truth of the situation was that the men knew more theology but we knew the teacher. At the time I thought the theological facts were irrelevant to my life, and I wondered how I would ever use anything I learned. As the years passed, I have come to the conclusion it was one of the most profitable classes I took at Messiah College. All my Bible courses have been very beneficial to me and I am so thankful Mr. Heisey insisted that I take them.

These courses were for me the beginning of seeing Scripture as more than facts. It was a practical guide for understanding Scripture and God. I know this was arranged by God because it has turned out to be one of the best things that happened to me and although not taught from the charismatic perspective it gave me the basis I needed to understand the deeper Spirit filled life that I experienced a number of years later. I realize now that God's hand was in this "mistake" in order to begin to prepare me for the experiences I would have in later life. One of the benefits was helping me see that we were created as a threefold being. I began to understand the difference of body, soul and spirit. Later I realized that in that class I had learned some basic truths that were important to understanding many other spiritual truths.

In chapter 12 we looked at the three areas of our life that are satan's targets for temptation. satan desires to prevent fruit and one of the ways he does this is by getting humans to be ignorant and confused by their body, soul and spirit. We must recognize that we are flesh people with an inborn sin nature, but God has provided through Christ the way to live in victory- not that we are perfect or will ever reach perfection in this world. We can learn, however, to win more than fail. As Christians we do not need to sin in word, thought and deed every day, as some people teach, but neither will we reach a point where we will be unable to sin.

satan is one source for temptation, but our own sinful nature also leads us into sin. A number of years ago there was a cartoon strip entitled "Pogo." Pogo, an alligator, if I remember correctly, was often in the middle of some battle. One day the cartoon showed Pogo meeting a friend before battle. He said to him, "We have found the enemy and it is us." As the saying goes sometimes we are our own worst enemy. Our body or flesh calls us loudly and satan will encourage us to listen to the flesh. Other people will sometimes encourage us or condone our actions. So we in a sense have three enemies- the world, satan and the flesh. We are responsible for our actions and cannot excuse our sin by blaming satan, the world or our human nature.

When I was teaching in Zimbabwe, Africa, sometimes a student would be found committing some wrong deed, like stealing school supplies or copying homework or test answers. When questioned why he did it, his favorite answer was, "The devil made me do it." It always reminded me of the comedian Flip Wilson who would use that line in one of his regular skits about Geraldine. The devil doesn't **make** us do anything. He suggests it and we yield to him or to our carnal nature. There is a way to become master of our carnal nature.

Previously the three parts of man were explained- body, soul and spirit. God has made provision for us to mature in each of these areas. As we develop and learn to control each of these areas of our lives, defeats will become less frequent.

We will never have more authority in the spiritual realm than we have authority over our own body and soul. Peter says in I Peter 2:11, "...I beseech you...abstain from fleshly lusts which war against the soul..." The word for "war" carries the idea of a soldier contending in battle. Peter teaches us that we are caught in a battle between our flesh and mind. We know a thing is wrong but our flesh wants to do it. When we are battling between what our body wants to do and what our mind tells us to do we open the door for satan to increase the temptation and suggest ways to fulfill hat sinful desire. Jesus said, "... a house divided against itself shall not stand." (Mat. 12:25) Although Jesus used this in reference to casting out demons by the power of satan, the principle is the same. Fighting temptation and sin on the purely body or flesh level or by my soul, mind and emotions will bring failure more often than victory.

Our body has desires that it sends to our emotions, will and mind. All of which are closely related. Our minds tell us that we ought not to do a certain thing but the body craves it. When we think of the word lasciviousness, we often consider it in the sense of immoral sexual behavior, but it is more than that. Lasciviousness and/or lust mean any overwhelming desire or craving. It is a very powerful and common struggle for many people, including Christians. Any physical drive that controls or drives us will usually find an ally in our soul and we face defeat. Our body and our soul join forces.

One day I am walking along and I see my favorite donut shop .My flesh/body tells me it is hungry, even though I ate a healthy breakfast. My eyes see how good the pastries look and my emotions remind me how much pleasure eating a donut always brings and my reasoning mind says it is okay to indulge myself a bit. I deserve it. MY spirit reminds me that I shouldn't eat a donut because I have had breakfast and don't need to indulge myself with coffee and donuts but I could give that bit of extra money to a Christian ministry. The battle begins. I lose my focus and I become a victim of my own making. satan knows he has gained a foothold into my life and will suggest I buy a whole dozen so that I will have one for a bedtime snack and tomorrow's breakfast and coffee break. Now this is an imaginary situation and somewhat oversimplified. It does help me to understand how we battle real temptations and sins. Eating donuts is not necessarily a sin.

Physical drives need to be kept in their proper place in order for us to grow spiritually. It is difficult, because often these lusts and actions stem from our childhood. I grew up in a home where good food was a sign of happiness, because it was most plentiful when we had company and holidays. The first thing planned for special events was the menu and it included special foods and drinks that were not readily available at any other time. Even today I can easily get caught up with that attitude. In fact I can make any day a special day if I plan good food!! This is just one form of lasciviousness. How do I learn to deal with it?

Scripture teaches us in Romans 6 that the body or old man nature is crucified with Christ that "...the body of sin might be destroyed, that henceforth we should not serve sin." It is a choice we must make. If the body is dead, why do I succumb to its demands?

Although God is willing to help, we also have to do our part to walk in obedience to Christ. God has given us a will and we make the choices. I choose what I will do or not do. Scripture tells me, "Put ye on the Lord Jesus Christ, and make not provision for the flesh, to fulfil the lusts thereof." (Rom. 13:14) The story is told about a young boy who lived in a house across from a farmer's field of watermelons. Day by day during the growing season the little boy watched the delicious melons develop. One day they looked ripe. His father saw the boy take a large sack and walk toward the field. The father asked the boy what he was doing. The boy replied that he was going to look at the melons and see if they were ripe. His father warned him against stealing and the boy said he knew it was wrong to steal. The father then questioned him further about the reason for the sack. The answer from the boy was that he was just taking it along because if he was tempted to steal he would have something in which to carry the melons.

We are instructed to "Mortify therefore your members which are upon the earth; fornication, uncleanness, inordinate affection, evil concupiscence and covetousness which is idolatry." (Col. 3:5) We have the choice to make, but God has provided help for us to choose correctly. What is God's help for us to master the flesh or body?

The way to win over the flesh is fasting. Fasting is a nasty word to most Americans today. It is easier to think "fats" than fast in our society for we are bombarded with ads for food, restaurants and snack shops. Although some medical doctors say it is not a good or healthy thing to do, fasting aids the body in several ways, if we are in normal health. When we think of fasting, perhaps we imagine going a week or longer without food, but there are all kinds and levels of fasting which we can follow.

First we want to see what God says about fasting. Jesus taught the concept of fasting. In Matthew 17 we read about a man who had a son that was a lunatic. He had taken that son to the disciples, but they were unable to cast out the demons. When this man came to Jesus, Jesus cast out the demons and restored the boy to normalcy. The disciples came to Jesus after this and privately asked Him why they could not cast out the demons. In verses 20 and 21 Jesus said, "...because of your **unbelief**...if ye have faith as a grain of mustard seed...nothing shall be impossible to you. Howbeit this **kind** goeth not out but by prayer and **fasting**." Notice the words in bold print- unbelief, kind and fasting. These are the key words. Jesus is not saying that when we fast we scare off demons. He is saying when we fast we stand up against unbelief. This "kind goeth out" is referring back to this kind of unbelief - the unbelief that hinders us from driving satan and demons away. Jesus told them that fasting builds faith!

In Matthew 9 we read another account about fasting. Some disciples of John came to Jesus and asked why His disciples did not fast as the Pharisees and they did. Jesus gave His answer in verse 15, "Can the children of the Bridegroom mourn as long as the Bridegroom is with them? But the days will come when the Bridegroom shall be taken from them, and then shall they fast." Jesus knew His disciples were still ignorant of His coming death and resurrection. He knew that when He was taken from them they would have to fast if they wanted to have faith to do great miracles. The day was coming when His followers would need faith not sight (His physical presence). Fasting would remove the unbelief that put a limit or cap on their lives. Today, as well, fasting removes the thing that keeps me from being all I can be. It gives power over the physical realm. We see this explained in Isaiah 58.

In the Old Testament we see that the people of Israel fasted, but often for the wrong reasons, like the Pharisees in Jesus' time on earth. In Isaiah 58 the Jews asked why their fasting was not seen by God. God responded through the prophet Isaiah, "Behold, ye fast for strife and debate and to smite with the fist of wickedness." The Hebrew meaning of that word strife means contention and actually comes from the root word for contest. They were trying to outdo each other in religious activities. They fasted to impress other people and when the fast was over they continued in disobedience to God. Isaiah continues under inspiration of God to explain the real purpose in fasting:

> "Is not this the fast that I have chosen? To loose the bands of wickedness, to undo the heavy burdens, and to let the oppressed go free, and that ye **break every yoke.**" (Is. 58:6)

The next verses state the purpose of fasting:

> "...that thou hide not thyself from thy own flesh. Then shall the light break forth as the morning and thine health shall spring forth speedily, and thy righteousness shall go before thee; the glory of the Lord shall be thy rereward (rear guard). Then shalt thou call and the Lord shall answer..." (Is. 58:7-9)

Fasting does not scare satan or impress God. It changes me by helping me see what I really am. It shuts down my flesh so that I can hear God speaking to me. The time I spend with God allows God to reveal Himself to me so that my faith in Him grows and He can then answer my prayers. It curtails my unbelief. It shuts down the flesh and shows the body who is in charge. It destroys the areas of my flesh that hinder me in my walk with God and enables me to resist flesh and body temptations. God has provided a way for us to be fruitful by physically fasting.

It would be wise to add that I am not saying you **must** go on a total fast. Let God direct in that. We can fast certain things we really enjoy. Stop eating chocolate or desserts. Give up drinking soda or coffee. Skip a whole meal once a week. You might even consider fasting something other than food. I have a friend who felt the Lord was telling her to quit reading so many Christian romance novels and spend time reading her Bible. A person could give up watching certain television programs-news or sports. If we pray God will give us direction. Start a little bit at a time. satan likes us to take on a type of fast that is too big for us to handle so that we quit and think we can't do it. I am not proposing fasting something that is already a sin and should not be in our lives. I knew a lady who said she always fasted for the season of Lent. She gave up using God's name in vain! That is not fasting. Fasting is not stopping something that is sin but giving up something you enjoy just for self disciplining the flesh. If you do have a certain behavior that is not sin in itself but is addictive that is a good place to start.

Last of all we can choose to master our body and soul by doing something that is good for us but we hate to do- like exercising regularly or eating a healthy food that you don't really like.

God has not only provided for the body to be mastered so that we can produce grapes but He has also provided healing for diseases and ailments of the body. It is not God's will for us to be sick. There were no diseases and sickness in the world God created for Adam and Eve. It is the devil and the fact that we live in a sinful world that brings illness. We know that when we are sick we are limited in worshiping and serving God. God provided healing in the death of His Son.

> "But He was wounded for our transgressions, He was bruised for our iniquities; the chastisement of our peace was upon Him and **with His stripes we are healed**." (Is. 53:5)

Notice the present tense of the verb "are", not can or will but **are**. Jesus' death on the cross provides physical healing as well as salvation. Some people have tried to tell me that this phrase does not refer to physical healing of the body, but this verse is quoted in the New Testament in Matthew 8:16, 17. In the evening many were brought to Jesus and "...He healed all that were sick; that it might be fulfilled which was spoken by Isaiah the prophet saying, "Himself took our infirmities and bare our sicknesses." Jesus is the same yesterday, today and forever so He made provision for the whole man, including our bodies. We can learn to conform to God's plan and find help to overcome our physical weaknesses in order to produce abundant fruit.

The provision for our soul, which is the mind, will and emotions, is the Word of God. Not just having a Bible that you carry to and read in church or keep on a table by your bed. It is more than reading your Bible through in a year or a set number of chapters a day or using a devotional book. It isn't memorizing Scripture. Memorizing Bible verses is a very helpful endeavor but unsaved people can quote verses. When I was teaching in a mission school in Zimbabwe, we had an African high school principal that encouraged Scripture memorization through an organization called Bible Memory Association. Yet he also would say to the students that **memorizing** the Word is not enough, because even some people in prison could quote Scripture. Even studying it to teach a Sunday School class or Bible study might be simply understanding the facts. Although each and every one of these things is good practice, we need to open our mind to let God speak a personal word and give understanding that applies to our lives. It is getting into the Word and letting God speak to me. Two Greek words for "word" are "logos" and "rhema." Logos is a communication in a general sense to all people who hear or read it, but rhema carries the idea of a personal word or command which applies to your life. We must not just read the Word as "logos" but let it become the revealed or personal word "rhema." from God. It is developing intimacy with God so that I can hear Him speak through the Word and let it change my way of thinking and acting. It must be alive. The Word needs to make my thinking new:

> "And be not conformed to this world; but be ye transformed by the **renewing** of your **mind**, that ye may prove what is that good and acceptable and perfect will of God." (Rom. 12:2)

There may be days when we read the Bible and don't get much from it, but reading daily must be a discipline before it becomes a joy. Sometimes I might be tired, but I read anyway. It is like canning or freezing fruits and vegetables. There are days when it just seems to be work, not much joy in doing it, but we know it will be stored away for future use. So we stay in the Word.

The Word builds our faith and makes it grow. It is in our minds to ward off fear and unbelief when problems come. "Faith comes by hearing and hearing by the Word of God." (Romans 10:17) It transforms us into Christ's image. The Word teaches and instructs us. It gives us light and direction, showing us the way to overcome difficulties in life. It teaches us about our authority in spiritual battles. It brings us emotional stability and peace because the Word is Jesus and Jesus is the Word. We need to learn to speak God's words, not our feelings or fears about a situation, "...The Word is nigh thee, even in the **mouth**, and in thy **heart**: that is the word of **faith**..." (Romans 10:8) When we speak God's promises it quiets our emotions against worry and fear. It makes us strong and fruitful. God responds to faith not fear. Jesus healed and said, "according to your **faith** be it done unto you." (Mat. 9:29) We are told to ask for wisdom but, ".let him ask in **faith**..." (Jas. 1:5, 6) We are told that "...without **faith** it is impossible to please Him..." (Heb.11:6) God made provision for my soul to be used to produce fruit. God said, "Let the word of God dwell in you richly..." That word "richly" means in abundance. We reap the quantity and quality of fruit to the degree we walk in the Word. It enables us to produce grapes and thus please God. In fact we are told that faith is the essence of our Christian walk, so it is a necessity to develop faith. In 2 Corinthians 5:7 we are told, "For we walk by **faith**, not by sight."

We have looked at God's way to victory in mastering our body and building our faith within our soul. Perhaps we can say that we are doing both these things, but what about our spirits? How do we develop our spirits to enable us to live the abundant fruitful life? God made provision for our spirits to be intimately connected to the Vine so we can produce delicious grapes.

Think about it

1. What are the three parts of man? Define the differences.

2. God is a triune God. Does each member of the trinity have all three parts - body (physical), soul (mind) and spirit?

3. What is the purpose and value of fasting? What is the relationship between fasting and faith and prayer?

4. Why is reading the Word important to us as Christians?

5. How do you develop a love for God's Word?

6. Do you have a plan to follow for reading the Bible? What would a beneficial plan for you?

Chapter 15

A Powerful Secret Nutrient That Increases Fruitfulness

Are we happy plastic people, under shiny plastic steeples?
With walls around our weakness and smiles to hide our pain
Is there anyone who's been there Are there any hands to raise?
Am I the only one who's traded in the altar for a stage?
The performance is convincing and we know every line by heart;
Only when no one is watching, Can we really fall apart?

These words from the song *Stained Glass Masquerade* by Casting Crowns depicts how I felt for a number of years after being saved. I knew all the verses and songs and followed all the church rules but I felt like I somehow needed and wanted more in my life. I can't say I was unhappy because I was very glad to be a Christian but I at times just wondered if there was something more. I would from time to time examine my life and wonder whether I was even producing the thirty-fold. I was seeking greater power and fulfillment in my life. I wondered about the gifts mentioned in Corinthians and knew some people were experiencing them, but I wasn't. Was there more that I was missing?

I had made friends with a teacher at Shalom and we were put together as class advisors. I enjoyed working with her. Over the summer we didn't see much of each other and when we came back to school one autumn I saw such a change in her that I wondered what had happened to her. This had happened once before when I was in Africa. When we went to Bulawayo to shop we often stopped at the home of a couple who served in a home for missionary children. One time I visited them and saw such a change in the wife that I knew something had happened to her. When I questioned her she tried to explain to me that she had received the infilling of the Holy Spirit. I didn't understand it and we did not see each other very often but I wanted what she had. Then when teaching at Shalom I saw a similar event in the life of my friend Debbie. I was really hungry to know God in this way. We had some good talks about it and one time she asked if she could pray with me. She prayed with me and when she got through she told me that God told her to tell me that He loved me. She was hesitant to tell me something so simple but she did. I could hardly believe those words. I had always, unknown to her, wondered if God **really** loved me or just loved everybody so was stuck with me. I did not receive the baptism of the Holy Spirit at that time but that night I went home and when I went to bed I asked God to fill me with the Holy Spirit with evidence of speaking in tongues. **He did!** It was something that has changed my life. Not that I am perfectly mature but I gained an inner strength and peace and enthusiasm about my Christian life. It was the power for growing in the spirit.

From God's Word we have seen how we can produce a more abundant harvest in developing the body and soul. The spirit is the third part of man and too many churches are not teaching how to make the spirit stronger. In fact some teach that man is only made up of two parts. They insist that the soul and spirit are the same and the two terms are used interchangeably. In theology it is called trichotomy (3 parts) or dichotomy (2 parts.) That was one of the lengthy often discussed and argued theological differences that came up in my Systematic Theology class. At that time I thought it was a waste of time because it really didn't seem to matter, but as I have learned more from the Word, I realize it is important to understand that man is three parts. It is a key to understanding many Scriptures and Biblical principles which help us to mature spiritually. If we cannot make our spirit stronger than our soul and body, we will always be limited in our Christian life.

When God created Adam and Eve they were threefold beings. Each part of their existence was in the right alignment with the spirit being the strongest influence. The relationship of the parts is illustrated below with the longest line showing the greatest controlling force;

spirit ------------------------------

soul ------------------

body --------

This is why it didn't matter that Adam and Eve were naked. They were controlled and motivated by their spirits and had no sin. They had a God given covering of glory. That is what is meant by Romans 3:23- "For all have sinned and come short of the **glory** of God." After Adam and Eve sinned, God provided animal skin covering "long coats (tunics)" for them. (Gen. 3:21 Amp) Man lost his glory covering when Adam and Eve sinned. However I believe we will receive a similar glory covering when we receive our glorious incorruptible bodies at our resurrection. We will not need man-made coverings. When Adam and Eve chose to be disobedient to God, they not only lost their godly glory covering, but their whole human character was distorted. We are now all born in this fashion:

spirit --------

soul ------------------

body ------------------------------------

Not only was the very nature of man distorted, but the whole world received a curse from their actions. There was a catastrophic change to all of God' creation that has continued up until this day and will do so until the millennium and eternity. Today we are born with our bodies in control. So little of life is in the spirit that we are basically spirit-dead. The spirit that is in a newborn child is formed and affected by its external circumstances which are basically evil. So the very sin nature of the child is quickly fed and catered to and the child is easily warped by its environment and its spirit is completely smothered by a sinful world. By school age the child has been bombarded by a flesh controlled world. The public schools ignore the spirit and teach the mind with some true facts but also many untrue ideas and false doctrines. We need to do all we can to encourage children to be sensitive to the spirit within them, because by the time most children reach adulthood they have lost sensitivity to spiritual things. This can happen even in Christian homes.

The spirit of man is his true nature and character as God created him, but the world ignores this part of man and actually attacks the spirit in its education of the mind or soul. Until man gets his immortal and incorruptible body, he will continue to have struggles. However God has redeemed man through Jesus' death and resurrection, "And you hath he **quickened** (revitalized, made alive) who were dead in trespasses and sins." (Eph. 2:1) and "...you, being dead in your sins and the uncircumcision of your flesh, hath he **quickened** together with him..." (Col. 2:13)

God through His Holy Spirit speaks to the spirit of man for God is a Spirit. God starts developing our spirit when we are saved because Christ revitalized us, but we must do our part to help our spirits to mature and become stronger so that we can be led by the Holy Spirit through our spirit. We need to understand that the words we hear and more importantly the words we say will affect our spirit. The words we speak and hear cause us to believe a certain way. Believing or thinking brings mindsets. If the facts are untrue we develop what Scripture calls "strongholds" These are incorrect patterns of thought that keep us in bondage. God speaks to our spirit in two ways- directly to our spirit and through His Word which can transform our way of thinking and believing. We are told that by reading God's Word we renew our minds. Then the Word affects our thinking and our thinking affects our believing and our believing affects what we say. God speaks to man's spirit, but our spirit cannot direct us if we have not learned how to listen to God and be in the Word to renew our mind and get it to line up with the spirit. The spirit of man must have the strongest voice.

In Galatians 5 we read concerning the battle of the flesh and spirit. Although various translations use a capital letter for "spirit" signifying the Holy Spirit it is not necessarily correct. In Greek there are no capitals and it uses just the word spirit. I believe it refers to man's spirit. We need to listen to our spirit and not our flesh for the two are opposites of each other and cause a battle within us. We need to recognize that the battle is within between the spirit, which wants to obey God and do right, and the soul/body that wants to please itself. Even the people of the world know that the battle between good and evil is within a man. The world calls it the conscience. If, as shown in the previous diagram, the flesh and soul are more in control than the spirit, which part of man will most often get its way?

When I was teaching high school I use to have students illustrate this battle. I would get three boys and label the biggest one "body", the middle-sized one "soul" and the littlest one spirit. Then I would ask if the body and soul took on the spirit which one would lose. They would agree the boy labeled spirit would. Then I would change the labels to the opposite so the biggest was "spirit." Again I would ask which one would win. They understood the lesson that the most developed boy won. Then I would go on to teach the importance of developing their spirits if they hoped to have victory in their lives. The lesson then was given on how to develop their spirits.

God did make provision to build a strong spirit within His children. I call it a secret, because it was many years before someone explained to me how to edify my spirit. The majority of churches do not teach this but the answer is found in the New Testament. In Jude 20 we read these words, "But ye, beloved, building up yourselves on your most holy faith, praying in the Holy Ghost." It must be the spirit man that is built up because the body needs to be made weaker by fasting and the soul(mind) is renewed and changed by the Word. So by praying in the Holy Ghost our spirit grows and matures. What does it mean to pray in the Holy Ghost or Spirit? God communicates with us through the spirit, not the body or soul. Job tells us:

"There is a **spirit** in man and the inspiration of the Almighty giveth them understanding." (Job. 32:8)

and:

"The **spirit** of man [that factor in human personality which proceeds immediately from God] is the lamp of the Lord, searching all his innermost parts. (Pr. 20:27) Amp.

Most of the time we pray using our mind, will and emotions, because God understands that part of us, but God speaks to our spirit and it then comes into our mind. So how do we pray in the spirit? Paul gives us the answer:

"For if I pray in an unknown tongue, my **spirit prayeth**, but my **understanding(mind)** is unfruitful." (I Cor. 14:14)

The fourteenth chapter of Corinthians and especially verse 14 is a point of much argument in the Christian church. The chapter deals with the subject of tongues, which is a highly controversial issue in Christianity. satan delights in this because he is the author of confusion and if he can keep tongues out of the church, he knows he is concealing a powerful tool that God gave the church. If satan cannot keep a church from believing and using tongues, he will try to bring an incorrect or improper use of them by getting people to use them for emotional display or a sign of being mature and causing tongues to be looked at with fear and suspicion.

There are extremes in the views of this gift by both those who believe in them and those who claim they are no longer for today. satan uses these emotions to cause church splits and keeps a powerful weapon that can be used against him from being used in the majority of mainline churches. We need to have an understanding of this gift and its uses. satan does not want us to be strong in spirit and live in victory over him. He is pleased if he can keep us in ignorance. If we do not open ourselves to the infilling of the Spirit it will keep us less fruitful and limit us in power in using the gifts for miracles and power.

In chapters 12 and 14 of I Corinthians, Paul is dealing with the topic of gifts and one of these gifts is tongues. God had Paul add the love portion (I Corinthians 13) to the middle of this discussion of gifts and tongues, because he was dealing with problems relating to the gifts, even in the early church. In discussing gifts it is important that we demonstrate love. Paul is giving instruction on the proper use of gifts which is using them in love and keeping them in right perspective. The use of gifts without love is of no value. Paul makes it clear to us that love is the basis for using the gifts, but they are to be used. There is no verse that tells us tongues are not for today or that they ended on a certain date or at a particular moment. The gifts are for the church to be used publicly and personally today as needs arise. We will be looking only at the gift of tongues, because it contains the secret of a lavish grape crop.

We need to understand that there are tongues for four different purposes. Notice in I Corinthians 12:10 it states "...divers kinds of tongues..." That means different languages will be used, some languages of this world but not known by the one speaking and others that are languages known only to God. It also means used in different ways with different purposes. Tongues have two uses for public ministry and two uses for private or personal practice.

Although this is not a chapter about tongues, it is important to discuss the various uses so we can understand how "praying in the Holy Ghost" edifies an individual.

In public, tongues are used as a sign for the unbelievers. This was demonstrated on the day of Pentecost, as recorded in Acts, when the Apostles received the gift of tongues to preach Christ as the Messiah and Savior to the people gathered in Jerusalem. That made it possible for unbelievers to hear in their own language Who Christ was. Paul quotes Isaiah 28:11 being fulfilled "...with men of other tongues and other lips will I speak unto this people...wherefore tongues are for a sign, not to them that believe, but to them that believe not..." (I Cor. 14:21, 22) I have heard of present day accounts of God using the gift of tongues in known human languages, but not known by the speaker. An evangelist I know was in a foreign country and preaching through an interpreter to an audience that did not know English. He felt inspired of God to begin to bring some words in tongues. As he waited for God to give him or someone else the interpretation, the interpreter looked at him strangely and asked him why, if he could speak the native language, did he not preach the whole message in it instead of using an interpreter. The Holy Spirit had given this evangelist the gift of an unknown (to him) tongue to be sure the people heard exactly what God wanted to say to them. The Holy Spirit gives the gift God wants to use in order to accomplish His will with the "...selfsame Spirit dividing to every man **as He wills...**"

The second use of tongues for public ministry is to give a word to minister to a group of believers in a public worship service. Paul clearly states that this message needs to be interpreted. In I Corinthians 14:27 Paul instructs the church, "If any man speak in an unknown tongue, let it be...by course, and let one interpret." In other words a message from God that comes to a believer in a public service is to be interpreted if it is to have any value. We stated before that God speaks to man's spirit and sometimes this comes via the Holy Spirit by tongues. This is one of the nine gifts of the Spirit listed in I Corinthians 12. Usually it is a prophetic word needed by a group gathered in a public service. An interrelation exists with three of the spiritual gifts-prophecy, tongues and interpretation of tongues.

For private or personal use tongues are for edification and intercession. Edification was discussed. Jude 20 instructs us to build ourselves up by praying in the Holy Spirit or in tongues. Tongues used in the prayer closet mature the spirit man and enables us to produce more grapes. It is God's provision to make us stronger in spirit so that we can "walk in the spirit." However closely related to praying to build my spirit strong is the ability to intercede for others. Paul charged the Ephesians, "Praying always with all prayer and supplication **in the spirit."** (Eph. 6:18) Praying in the spirit is the term commonly used for praying in tongues either for self edification or intercession. Paul writes in I Corinthians 14:14, "For if I pray in an unknown tongue, my **spirit prayeth...**" In charismatic circles prayer in the spirit or in tongues is called using one's "prayer language." Most of us Christians have experienced a heavy burden of prayer coming upon us for a situation or problem and we run out of words to pray. This is when praying in the spirit or in one's prayer language is so helpful. There is another advantage to praying in tongues and that is that God knows and understands but not other people, or satan or any of his demons. satan will have a harder time hindering answers when he doesn't know what we are asking God to do.

> "... for he that speaketh in an unknown tongue speaketh not unto men, but unto God; for no man understandeth him; howbeit in the spirit he speaketh mysteries." (I Cor. 14:2)

Confusion often comes over the use of tongues because people do not understand all the variety or purposes for tongues. Also some churches and denominations see tongues as a sign to others that they have reached a great level of maturity. A baby Christian can receive the gift of tongues as a prayer language. Tongues for personal use are not a sign of maturity but rather a tool to use to grow and mature.

Having a prayer language also enables the Christian to worship more freely. Our prayer language can be used in worship of God in private. However in some churches during worship time tongues will be used for public worship or in singing as a congregation. This is called singing in the spirit and is a beautiful form of praise and worship. Jesus told the woman of Samaria that the day was coming that, "...the true worshipers shall worship the Father in spirit..." (Jn. 4:23)

When a person receives his/her prayer language he/she will be filled with fervor and enthusiasm, but not maturity. It is similar to a young person who gets their high school diploma or college degree. They are excited and are sure they are the next great world celebrity, but they have only gained certain tools and opened the door to enter the real world and grow up. Tongues are a tool to maturity and the opening of the door for the Holy Spirit to let the nine gifts flow through them **"as He wills."** There should be no more pride in having received a prayer language than being born again. It is the beginning of something not the end. We need to understand that tongues for personal prayer are available for use anytime by the Spirit filled Christian but tongues for public ministry are not.

Another confusing issue with tongues that churches have, because of not understanding the use of tongues for personal and public ministry, is the misuse of a quote from I Corinthians 12:30. They read "...do all speak with tongues? Do all interpret?" The answer from the context of the passage is "no." That is the correct answer because Paul is dealing here with the public use of gifts, and not all Christians who have a prayer language will necessarily have a word for a public meeting. We must understand that ALL the gifts in this chapter are for personal use as well as public ministry. It is like any other portion of Scripture. Every verse in the Bible is meant for the church but it is also meant for us personally! Tongues for personal use in prayer and intercession can be had by all God's children.

There is another valuable benefit in praying in tongues. The following article from Oral Roberts University in Tulsa was given out at a Kenneth Copeland meeting. Dr Carl Peterson, a brain specialist, did research on the relationship between the brain and praying in tongues:

> Through the research and testing Dr Peterson found that, as we pray in the spirit or worship in the spirit, there is activity that begins in our brain. As we engage in our heavenly language, the brain releases two chemical secretions that are directed into our immune system, giving a 35 to 40 percent boost to our immune system. This promotes healing in our bodies. Amazingly this section is triggered from a part of the brain that has no other apparent activity in humans. It is only activated by our spirit-led prayer and worship. (ThruLife.net)

God is no respecter of persons. He would not enable one Christian to have a tool for worship, intercession, and edification in order to mature and refuse to give it to another. Many churches teach good Biblical truths about mastering the body and maturing the soul, but fail to teach how to build a strong spirit because they do not believe in the gifts and tongues. This is a teaching ignored, misunderstood and feared by many denominations.

The secret of "fertilizing" our spirits so that they grow in power is allowing God to fill us with His Holy Spirit, which opens us up to operate in the fullness of the gifts that have been promised to us in I Corinthians 12. God is willing and waiting to lead us into this experience for it is a step which will enable us to be all God wants us to be. It will enable us to become stronger spiritually, to more clearly hear God speak to us and open the door to use the gifts and operate in miracles, signs and wonders. It is the way to receive the anointing to fulfill the calling God has on our lives and be used as a part of His body for reaching a lost world.

So how do I receive this prayer language to mature in spirit and to be used by God for the supernatural? I must receive the baptism of the Holy Spirit. This is the anointing with the oil of the Holy Spirit. This will make an abundant life.

Think about it

1. Which part of man should be the strongest force? What provision has God made for it to be strong?

2. What are the four purposes for tongues?

3. Can a Christian operate in the gifts of I Corinthians 12 without the baptism of the Holy Spirit?

4. What are the purposes of the gifts and are they needed today?

5. How can we learn to hear God and be used in the powerful gifts?

Chapter 16

Fruitfulness Through the Holy Spirit

At Shalom Academy there was a small storage room with a work table at one end and some chairs where we teachers could sit and work when we had a break from teaching. There was a copier there as well as other school supplies. One day I went down there to do some work and the music teacher was there. We started talking and in the course of the conversation he asked me to explain what the baptism of the Holy Spirit was. As I was explaining it to him another teacher walked in and she joined the conversation by saying she didn't really believe in such a thing and she was so content with her Christian life that she didn't need anything more. I had no desire to argue with anyone about this experience. Our teachers came from different theological backgrounds and my job was not to go around teaching mine, so the music teacher walked out and the conversation changed. After a few minutes the lady teacher started talking about her husband and how wonderful he was and how good it was to be married. I believe the Lord gave me the words to say at that time. I told her that I did not see any need for marriage for me because I was quite content being single. She responded back quickly that I could not talk from experience of marriage. She had been single and married so she knew the joys of marriage. I simply answered by saying that that was the same way with the baptism of the Holy Spirit. She made a few feeble excuses and some reasons why she felt it was not Biblical and then left the room. I knew the reality of the baptism just as she knew the reality of a good marriage. We are still friends but don't see each other very often since neither of us is teaching at Shalom Academy now.

We want to look at Scripture and see if the baptism of the Holy Spirit is Biblical.

There are three different types of baptism recorded in the New Testament. The first occurs when we accept Christ as our personal Savior. When we do this we are baptized into Christ's body according to Scripture:

> "For as many of you have been **baptized into Christ**, have put on Christ." (Gal. 3:27)

> "For by one Spirit we are all **baptized into one body**." (I Cor. 12:13)

> "Know ye not, that so many of us as were **baptized into Jesus Christ** were baptized into his death." (Rom. 6:3)

The second type of baptism is water baptism. This is the proper step for a new convert to take as a public demonstration of his decision to follow and walk in obedience to God. Jesus Himself was baptized in water as an adult. In Acts 2:28 Peter preached "...Repent and be baptized." Many times we have accounts of water baptism after an individual accepted Christ. The Ethiopian eunuch and the jailer at Philippi were each baptized after believing in Christ. Most Christian churches practice water baptism, however, there are no examples in the Bible of infant baptism but rather dedication of babies and water baptism after conversion. Churches are familiar and teach these first two baptisms. What about the third type of baptism? It is ignored by many Christian mainline denominations.

The baptism of the Holy Spirit is the third Biblical baptism for believers. After Jesus' death and resurrection, He appeared to His disciples several times. In John 20 we read that Jesus appeared to the disciples gathered together. If we look at verses 21 and 22 we read these words:

"Then said Jesus to them again, 'Peace be unto you: as My Father hath sent me, even so send I you.' And when he had said this, he breathed on them, and saith unto them, 'Receive ye the Holy Ghost." (Jn. 20:21, 22)

Did the disciples receive the Holy Spirit into their lives at that time? If Jesus said it was to happen, it surely did and the disciples did receive the Holy Spirit into their lives. They were born anew. In the Amplified Bible verse 23 says this: "Now **having received** the Holy Spirit and being led and directed by Him..." This would make one conclude that they had received as Jesus commanded. This was before the Day of Pentecost. Why then do we read these words in Acts?

"...wait for the promise of the Father which, saith He, ye have heard of me. For John truly baptized with water, but ye shall be baptized with the Holy Ghost not many days hence...But ye shall receive power after that the Holy Ghost is come upon you..." (Acts 1:4, 5, 8)

These disciples **received** the Holy Spirit in their receiving Christ being baptized into Christ, but Jesus told them to gather and not depart but "wait for the promise of the Father" because "John truly baptized with water, but ye shall be baptized with the Holy Ghost." They had been baptized in to Jesus' body but they needed the "baptism of the Holy Spirit. When Jesus appeared to His disciples after His resurrection he said, "Receive ye the Holy Spirit." (John 20:22) If Jesus said it happened and if that were the complete work of the Holy Spirit in the Christian's life why did He tell them to go and wait for the Holy Spirit? These Scriptures clearly show that receiving the Spirit at the new birth is not the same as being baptized in the Spirit.

Individuals and churches who deny this "second work of the Spirit" will quote a verse from Romans 8:

"But ye are not in the flesh, but in the Spirit, if so be that the **Spirit of God** dwell in you. Now if any man have not the **Spirit of Christ,** he is none of his." (Rom. 8:9)

The part they quote is the last phrase stating "if any man have not the **Spirit of Christ**, he is none of his." If a person is saved he has the Spirit of Christ. That is true. That is the baptism referred to in the beginning of this chapter- baptized into the body of Christ. There is more. This verse also talks about the "Spirit of God." Why did the writer use two different phrases?

There is an important view of the trinity that very few people teach. God is a trinity, that is Father, Son Jesus, and Holy Spirit. Yet each of these individuals is also triune beings. God is a Spirit (Jn. 4:24) and God has a soul (mind, will, emotions). God loves, hates, has thoughts and creates. But God also has a physical body. Jacob said he saw God "face to face" which in the Hebrew can carry the idea of seeing a part of someone (Gen. 32:30) and Moses saw a part of God (Gen. 33:13-23). Christ also is a spirit (Rom. 8:9), has a soul (mind, will, emotions) (Ph. 2:5; Matt. 6:39; Jn. 11:5), and He has a body (Jn. 20:27). The Holy Spirit is a spirit and He has a soul. John14:26 says He teaches so He has a mind. (Although I must admit I had a few teachers in my life that seemed to have lost their mind.) Eph. 4:30 says He has emotions and John 16:13 shows He has a will but is obedient to the Father. The Holy Spirit also has physical form (Lk. 3:22). Therefore we see that God has a spirit and Christ has a spirit. We receive Christ's spirit at our spiritual birth (as the disciples did in John 20) to be reborn and know we are going to get eternal life but we need to receive God's spirit for the power (Acts 1 and 2) to serve Him and win more souls for the kingdom and to operate in the gifts of I Cor. 12.

Let me repeat these important facts. Christ breathed upon His disciples and said "Receive ye the Holy Ghost." That was the initial step of becoming a Christian. When we become a Christian, that is when we receive the Spirit of Christ. Then Jesus told them to "...wait for the promise of the **Father**" On the Day of Pentecost the believers in the upper room received the "Spirit of God" in a second step known by Jesus' words- "ye shall be baptized with the Holy Ghost not many days hence." So we today wait and believe and receive the Spirit of the Father in an experience called the baptism of the Holy Spirit. The baptism of the Holy Spirit is receiving the **Spirit of God**.

If we read verse 9 in context of the entire eighth chapter of Romans this will be confirmed. This passage was addressed to Christians. They had the spirit of Christ because they had been born again, but they are carnal Christians walking in their flesh - Christians who follow the body and soul inclination. Then in verse 9 he concludes that we are not in the flesh walking after its urges but are walking in the Spirit if ".the Spirit of God dwell in you." The baptism of the Holy Spirit makes a difference. To illustrate these two steps imagine yourself as an empty water glass. When you get saved your glass is filled with the Spirit of Christ. The glass is filled and controls the water- where it goes or sits. The person is a Christian and controls where he goes or sits, because he is still controlled by soul and body not completely by the Spirit(water). The baptism of the Holy Spirit is like placing the water glass into water- plunging it down into the basin. There is still water in the glass but the water surrounding the glass can control the glass. That is the difference. The Father baptizes or plunges me into His Spirit and I have the power (that's what Jesus said-but ye shall receive power) to mature and train my soul and body to do what and go where He leads me. We are not made perfect but we are able to function in the gifts of I Corinthians 12 and minister better to other people and to find inner strength/power to hear God speak and to obey. Also to have an intimate prayer language.

In my desire to make it clear that this experience is Biblical I realize I have repeated statements. I have tried to explain it in various ways because it is an important step for the Christian walk. The devil hates us to take this step and to have a prayer language that he cannot understand. That is why he gets churches and denominations to deny it or argue over it- anything to keep it out of the life of a Christian.

The power of this baptism lies in our ability to pray in the spirit or in tongues. That is what edifies us and helps us to mature. It brings us into a closer intimate relationship with God and makes us more sensitive to God and enables us to hear Him more clearly. Having a prayer language is not a sign of maturity. It does not make me superior or more spiritual. It is a tool to help me mature.

It is like the marriage ceremony for a couple. The ceremony isn't the marriage. It doesn't make a mature marital relationship. It is only the initial step into a marriage relationship that will take time to grow and mature.

With the infilling of the Spirit also comes more sensitivity in the use of the spiritual gifts of I Corinthians 12. The Spirit desires to use these gifts in the church today. The maturing of our spirit empowers us to operate in the gifts for ministry to others or for the church body or even for our own personal needs. Time praying in the spirit helps us to know God's voice and not satan's voice or our own flesh.

Some Christians and churches overemphasize tongues at the exclusion of the other gifts. Remember being filled with the Spirit and being able to speak and/or pray in tongues is not a final goal, but a step along the way. The purpose and use of this gift was more fully explained in chapter 15. Are tongues more important that the other gifts in I Corinthians 12? What is the most important gift? The most important gift is the one needed to meet a particular need at a particular time. If I need healing, tongues is not the gift I need. I need the gift of healing.

However the use of tongues, even as a public gift is probably the easiest in which to function, so if I can't even believe God for a prayer language or for a public word in tongues, I will probably find it very difficult to allow the Spirit to work though me in the other gifts. Someone once explained it this way- tongues is the entry level gift. The need is to be baptized with the Holy Spirit and to receive a prayer language in order to mature.

In Acts every time a person or persons were filled with the Spirit they gave evidence of it with the sign of tongues. It is the assurance of the Spirit's filling. It happened at Pentecost as recorded in Acts 2:1-4. We read in Acts 8 where the people of Samaria accepted Christ and were baptized in water after receiving Christ (Acts 8:12) and later received the baptism by the Spirit in Acts 8:14-17. It does not say they spoke in tongues but it does say that "Simon **saw** that through the laying on of hands that the Holy Ghost was given. What did Simon see? What was the manifestation of the baptism? Speaking in tongues.

Also in Acts 10:44-46 at Cornelius' house they heard them speak with tongues, and magnify God. This brings to our attention that our prayer language is a wonderful way to praise God, as well as for edification and intercession. In Acts 19:1-6 we read that at Ephesus the believers also spoke with tongues and used it to prophesy.

Any Christian who desires to be Spirit filled may receive the baptism and a prayer language for personal edification, intercession and praise. Being filled is as simple as being saved. We simply believe it is for me and ask. Here are some practical steps to help you:

1. Believe it is for you and ask God to fill you with His Spirit. Luke 11:9-13, especially verse 13 "How much more will your heavenly Father give the Holy Spirit to them that ask him."

2. After asking for the Spirit speak no English. Be quiet before God and allow unspoken thanksgiving and praise fill your mind.

3. Relax and breathe deeply as if breathing in the Spirit and when a strange word or phrase comes to your mind, speak it aloud. At first it may sound strange but repeat it offering it as praise to God. As other words come, use them aloud and freely. Mark 16:17 "And these signs shall follow them that believe; in my name they shall cast out devils; they shall **speak with new tongues**."

In the Old Testament circumcision was practiced as a sign of Israel's covenant with God. In the term "making" a covenant, the Hebrew actually uses the word "cutting." There had to be the shedding of blood in some way. The study of covenants is very rewarding and enlightening, but all I will say here is that circumcision was a symbol of a covenant involving the male reproduction organ. This is significant in that God was using human reproduction to birth the Savior to redeem the world. It was using physical actions to achieve a spiritual goal. In the New Testament we are to reproduce spiritually. To do that the organ we need to use is the tongue. Our tongues need a type of circumcision for they are called an unruly organ. It is a world of iniquity and defiles. God's way of helping us to tame our tongue and get excited about sharing Christ with a lost world is through the power of the baptism of the Holy Spirit. Old Testament circumcision is a symbol of New Testament tongues and prayer language, a setting apart by the infilling of the Holy Spirit. God has made provision for His children to produce abundant fruit.

The baptism of the Holy Spirit is not only a Biblical reality but can be real in the life of every born again Christian to enable us to pray and minister more powerfully and effectively. It is not a required step to get to heaven, but it is a maturing step for producing more fruit for God.

It is like the story of the man who lived in Europe and wanted to reach the United States. He finally saved enough money for passage on a ship. He got on the ship and spent most of his time in his room. When he got hungry and smelled the delicious food being served in the dining room he would eat a few of the crackers he had brought with him. He even went out once and peeked at the tables filled with trays of luscious food. At last he arrived in the States and was getting off the ship and the captain was saying goodbye to the passengers. The captain looked at this man and said he had never seen him before and asked where he had been. The passenger sadly admitted he had stayed in his room because he had only enough money for his passage and no money for the meals. When the captain explained that the meals came with the ticket, the man was sorry he had lived on plain crackers when so much was available to him that had been paid for. He reached his destination but missed some of the pleasures along the way. That's how it is when we Christians are ignorant of the fullness of the Spirit or deny its reality. We will make it to our destination but we will miss some of the joys and benefits on the journey.

God has made provision for our spirits to be strong by providing a prayer language and it is possible for me and everyone who simply reaches out in faith to receive it. We have seen that this baptism of the Spirit is one of three baptisms mentioned in Scripture and can be ours in a few easy steps.

Think about it

1. What are the three different baptisms mentioned in Scripture?

2. Are all three baptisms meant for all people?

3. Does operating in the gifts make us more fruitful? Are the gifts themselves fruit?

Chapter 17

Pruned Branches Produce More Fruit

One of the challenges for a missionary going to a foreign country is learning the language of the country where you have been called. Some seem to be more adept at learning languages than others but everyone makes mistakes. When someone is learning English and makes a mistake, I can laugh and think it is cute or funny, but when I make the mistake in a foreign language I am usually embarrassed.

Some mistakes are minor and the people you are talking to will ignore them because they know what you mean, but others can be very embarrassing. One time I was opening the Sunday School before the students were dismissed for their individual classes. I got the words for open and close turned about and we closed when we started and opened when they left for class. No one laughed or did what I said but followed the proper pattern and it was all over before I was told I made the error. That was not too serious.

Another time I was talking in a language class to our African language teacher and he was having us give testimonies to practice the Ndebele language. All of a sudden he got all embarrassed and looked away. I asked him what I had said and he said he could not tell me because it was not nice. Perhaps it was good he didn't.

At that same session another missionary lady wanted to give her testimony and she said she wanted to be an ambassador for Christ, but by adding one more syllable to the word for ambassador she said- I want to be a **motorcycle** for the Lord. In our mistakes our African teacher would correct us, but do it gently in a way to help us not to discourage or hurt us.

Correction is necessary in our lives in many areas and some is easier to take than others. Even when God needs to correct us it might be an easy adjustment, but most of the time it is hard to respond with joy.

God is good. He is both merciful and gracious. Someone once told me a wonderful way to remember the difference between God's mercy and grace. Mercy is God **not** giving us what we **do** deserve and God's grace is giving us what we **do not** deserve. God is the giver of good gifts. Scripture tells us "every good and perfect gift is from above, and cometh down from the Father of lights..." (Jas. 1:17) God does not mistreat His children. That would be child abuse and God isn't guilty of that, but He will correct us when we need it.

As we saw before in Luke 11 it tells us that if evil people know how to give good gifts, how much more does God give good things. However we often see that bad things happen to good people. The bad things do not come from God, but He does allow them because He is bound by spiritual laws.

I do not claim to understand all these laws, particularly in relation to what satan is permitted to do on earth, but I do know that satan and his demons cause bad events. The three basic sources of sin and tragedy are satan, the world (and those in it) and me myself.

It is easy to blame every bad work on satan, but he is under spiritual laws of limitation and is only one source of our problems. The world is evil and indirectly that is a result of satan, but satan can use people to create difficult and evil situations. satan is allowed to attack and to tempt people. If we consider the Apostle Paul we read how he had received a messenger of satan to buffet him. We know he also suffered many beatings and persecutions at the hands of the people (the world) and God allowed it. He allows both Christians and non-Christians to make choices and to do evil for He created man with free will.

However a lot of our troubles come from our own choices. If we are disobedient to God's laws, either natural or spiritual, (and we can choose to be) then we can expect to experience the consequences of that disobedience. God doesn't put bad things on people because they sinned, e.g. AIDS, but He tells us not to do certain things because they will result in trouble and difficulties for us like aids. Many people see aids as God's punishment for perverted sexual lifestyle, but God told us not to live that way because He knew that it would bring diseases to us. Sin always has terrible consequences. We need to understand that God has given His Word to guide us so that we can avoid the hurtful suffering that will come if we choose to sin, but God is merciful when we repent. He will forgive us. How much better it is when we follow His Word in order to avoid sin and its injurious consequences. He has also given us instruction on how to overcome evil when it comes from either the world or satan.

When we buy a new car we are given a manual of instructions. We can choose whether to read and follow it or ignore it. That manual tells us what to do to take care of our car, but if we refuse to do as it suggests there will be problems. When the oil isn't checked or changed as directed and the car stops functioning, it is useless to blame the car dealer or maker. It is our fault. God's manual to us is His Word. We can follow it or choose to ignore it, but when everything goes wrong God is not to blame anymore than the car dealer.

God clearly instructs us by telling us what is sin, but there are many other things that are neither good nor bad within themselves that we can use the way we choose. We can misuse or overuse legitimate things, making them sinful. For example, a computer is not sinful but if we use it to obtain pornography it becomes sinful. Television is not evil but we can watch things that are sinful and can cause us to sin. A gun can be used to shoot an animal to supply us with food or can be used to rob a grocery store to get food and possibly shoot the owner.

There are many things that are neither good nor evil in themselves but we can use them to excess or allow them to become more important to us than we should. They may be unnecessary things or they may eventually become sin to us. These are the kinds of things that need pruning from our lives.

Grape vines must be pruned to produce good grapes. I find it difficult to prune my grapevine. It is hard to cut back some of the branches that look healthy, but it is necessary so that the branches are not crowded. Sometimes you can find a branch that seems to be growing wildly or even one that has been broken. Pruning is necessary if you want to get fruit.

There is also a process of pruning that is necessary in our lives. To produce fruit we must be pruned. We can get our lives too busy and overcrowded and God asks us to give up things that are not necessarily sinful in themselves.

One of my friends told me that God asked her to give up reading so many novels. They were Christian books but God wanted her to spend less time reading fiction and spend more time in the Word and fellowshipping with Him. This was an act of pruning by God to make her more fruitful.

God will talk to us gently to prune back the things He wants us to surrender to Him, but if we ignore that voice He will allow us to go our own way and let us become fruitless. However when we do ignore God we usually open ourselves to satan and his devices and bad things happen to us. God will use these bad things to prune us, but it is much better to allow God to do the pruning directly.

In the book of Hebrews we learn about the Lord's chastening. This is God's way of pruning and crushing to make sweet grapes and wine. The writer of Hebrews tells the Christians:

> "Now no chastening for the present seemeth to be joyous, but grievous: nevertheless afterwards it yieldeth the peaceable fruit of righteousness." (Heb. 12:11)

God's correction comes to the spirit or heart of man. God does not **give** sicknesses and diseases to correct us. God can use the time of sickness or disease to speak to individuals, but He speaks to man's spirit. God's chastening is not an attack against our bodies. God does not put diseases on His children anymore than you would on your children. However when we have physical problems God will talk to us and use them to try to correct us. God works lovingly with us in grace and mercy and will do so until the final day of judgment.

The Greek word for chastening carries a positive concept of instruction or nurturing discipline. It is a teaching to correct a harmful behavior or attitude. The writer of Hebrews compares discipline in the earthly manner from earthly fathers to the "Father of spirits." Of course, there are cruel earthly fathers who have misused discipline but a loving earthly father disciplines for our good. This correction is a physical outward correction with limited physical applications, but we call it child abuse if the discipline is actually harmful to a child's body or causes lifelong emotional consequences. Just as an earthly father uses the physical things of the world to correct us, so our spiritual Father uses the spiritual realm for His correction God is always gentle yet clear in His teaching and guiding us. He speaks to our spirits. We commonly use the term our conscience. He convicts us when we do wrong or need to make changes in our lives.

God does this to make us more fruitful. This is the pruning process so we can produce more and sweeter fruit. As stated earlier God can **use** physical suffering as a time to talk to the spirit of man, because hard times often drive a person to God. However the correction of God is always a spiritual one meant for our good. According to Jesus' words:

> "Every branch in me that beareth not fruit he taketh away; and every branch that beareth fruit, he purgeth it, that it may bring forth more fruit." (Jn. 15:1)

The word "purge" comes from the Greek root word that means to make clean. God wants us to be pure. Jesus explains how we are purged or made clean in verse 2 of this fifteenth chapter of John, "Now ye are clean through the Word..." God prunes and convicts us on a purely spiritual level as we spend time with Him and His Word.

We can choose to change our ways when God speaks or we can choose to ignore His voice. If we do not make the necessary changes God will allow (in fact He must allow) satan access to our physical body. Paul gives an example of something similar in I Corinthians 5. A man was in sin and Paul told the congregation that they must deliver this man into the hands of satan for an attack on the flesh in order to save his soul. God would not correct via the physical.

We need to know that God does allow satan to tempt and trouble us in line with His spiritual laws. As was said before satan has certain limited authority on this earth. An example of this is when Jesus cast the demons out of Legion and the demons asked to not be sent out of the country but to be sent into a herd of swine and Jesus did that. Perhaps someday we will understand that.

It is true that most correction is unpleasant. We do not like to change or give up certain bad habits, but we need to keep in mind that although temporarily it may hurt, in the end it brings us joy and blessing. We need to always focus on the end results and purposes of God. Learning to listen to God carefully will make pruning less difficult, and it will help us avoid the things that hinder us spiritually.

When we are going through a difficult time we need to take time to seek God and allow Him to show us the cause of the problem(s.) Many times they are of our own making and God will correct us and help us to change. We need to realize that God is pruning us to make us stronger.

What we need to keep in mind when we are facing issues is to be sure we are walking in obedience to God and the problem is not self-made. Then listen to God to understand how He wants to refine us. Then we will bear more fruit.

We need to remember that just as pruning is not only good but necessary to make a vine produce profusely, so our lives too can benefit from pruning. God will try to prune us, but if we fail to allow Him to do the work He desires, He will use the trials that come from other sources to prune us.

Someone once said that dying to my own wants and desires and becoming more Christ like is similar to peeling an onion. It comes off a layer at a time with lots of tears. It may not be pleasant and it can bring tears at time but the pruning is for my benefit to make me more fruitful. God may even choose to use me as wine, but that takes squeezing and crushing.

Pruning by God is for our good. It is discipline given on the spiritual level. God does not give us diseases and physical punishment but if we keep moving stubbornly forward and refuse to listen problems will come and God will use those problems to help us yield to His way. We need to always remember that God's ultimate end is for our good and when we submit to Him we will find great joy even if the change is difficult at first. We will also realize that the taking away of certain things from our lives will turn into a blessing for us because we will become branches of bountiful fruit.

Think about it

1. Why does God prune us?

2. How does God prune us?

3. How should I respond to correction from God? From other people?

4. What will happen in my life if I resist pruning?

5. Share a personal lesson of pruning in your life, if you can.

Chapter 18

Crushed Fruitfulness

Every year Shalom Christian Academy (the school where I taught for 25 years) has a wonderful weekend called Dutch Fest. The parents, students, staff and the administration all help to make it possible. It is the major fund raiser for the school. The goal is to raise over one hundred thousand dollars to enable the school to meet its annual budget. Although a lot of the work is done the week before the sale; there is work all through the year to do the necessary planning, organizing and making of goods to be sold. One of the events is a homemade quilt sale.

During the weeks before the sale mothers and grandmothers can be found sitting in the entry hall of the school finishing the quilting. Some of the ladies that come have small preschool children who play nearby. One day another teacher and I went to the office which looks out on the entry hall and saw a group of children playing, while their mothers were quilting. One little girl had taken charge of the rest telling them how and what to play. This other teacher made the comment that that child was very bossy. As I watched I told this teacher I didn't think she meant to be bossy but was using (or rather misusing) her gift of organization that we read about in Romans 12.

The gifts we read about in Romans 12 are inborn or inherent gifts. They can be found in unsaved people as well as Christians. They can be spotted in very young children. They are given to us by God at the time of our conception. They are commonly called talents. Every person has been given one or more of these gifts to use as they choose. The majority of unsaved people misuse them and even Christians can misuse their inborn gift. Not only children but adults often misuse them.

My sister lived next to a lady that had the gift of mercy but she was not a Christian and used this gift to take in every stray dog or cat and even picked up birds that had been hurt and took them to the veterinarian to try to save them. She would feed squirrels and mice and rabbits. However when it came to people she could be very nasty, even to her own family. We have unsaved individuals that have a gift of giving but again use it for unimportant things like saving trees and weeds.

What is sad is that even as a Christian I can fail to recognize these gifts in myself and misuse them selfishly or wrongly. That is why we need God's Spirit in us. We are all different and have a special purpose and that is why God made us like He did.

If we just look at our own actions as well as the actions of others we soon see that we are born in sin, because all of us are guilty of misusing our innate abilities given by God. Even the fact that God created man to have dominion on earth is warped into control and manipulation of people and animals rather than the original purpose for dominion and authority. This misuse is seen in a variety of people with differing gifts, backgrounds cultures and colors. There are no two individual humans exactly alike, not even identical twins. Every person has his or her unique fingerprints. God is so creative that there are not even two snowflakes alike. God has made us all different because He has a purpose and place for us in His plan. God seems to like variety.

Grapes, too, come in a variety of types and colors. They may be black, blue, purple, red, green or even white. Grapes are nutritious in all forms. Grapes can be eaten fresh or be used for raisins, jelly, juice or wine. Although I have never developed a taste for wine, doctors say drinking it in moderation has certain benefits. Wine can be used for medicinal purposes. It can bring healing and health. Misuse of wine, however, does just the opposite. Some of the fruit we produce as Christians is like wine. It brings healing and health, but the things that come out of us as Christians can be unhealthy and hurtful.

Wine is used to stimulate appetite. Some wines are hearty, others are delicate. Some are sweet and rich while others are sparkling and bubbly. Each variety of grapes is cultivated for a specific purpose. We are also each made for a purpose. God has created us with our own individual blend of gifts and personalities. We need to allow God to produce the fruit He wants in us to be used as part of His plan. There are no accidents in humans. We are who God made us and as a poster I used to have states – God does not make junk! However we need to allow God to develop these gifts or they become perverted. This takes time for growing and maturing.

The making of wine takes time. It takes time to grow the grapes and more time to age the wine. During the aging process, wine is filtered a number of times to remove all the impurities. This is a good parallel for us. We must give God time and allow Him to filter out impurities to make us a quality person "fit for the kingdom of God."

We are born with gifts but it takes time for us to develop them and to let God refine them into high quality use. Each of the gifts listed in Romans 12 can be used for good or evil. These are basic gifts given to each person at birth. Even unsaved individuals have these gifts but do not use them in a godly way. They have a gift of teaching but use this powerful tool to teach counterfeit doctrines and beliefs. They have a gift for organizing and organize marches for gay rights. They even have a gift to make money but misuse it.

Some Christians have no idea of what their gift or gifts are. The gifts we receive are meant to be used for the calling God has on our lives. We need to have a good understanding of the gifts described in Romans 12. If we do not recognize our abilities or gifts we can spend our entire life serving in a ministry not meant for us. That is sad for God has given everybody at least one gift and most people have several.

I have known people who never used their gifts at all because they thought they had none. Others are somehow convinced they have a certain gift for teaching or helping and do not and spend their energies doing things God didn't intend for them to do. I know people who thought they had a gift for teaching and volunteered to teach Sunday School but bored their classes so that people stopped attending Sunday School when they knew that person was going to teach. I know of other individuals who had the gifts for the calling of evangelist, but they did not understand that and took on pastorates. God cannot help us produce fruit if we transplant ourselves into the wrong soil. It would be like planting a vineyard in a dry desert area and hoping that somehow it would bring forth grapes and wine.

When someone moves into an area not meant for them it not only hinders their fruit but takes away the spot where God wanted to plant someone else. The church must teach us how to identify our gifts and callings if we expect Godly fruit to come forth. There are many tests for people to take to help them find their gift but many are confusing, because people mix the gifts of Romans 12 (which are given to us to use as we choose) with the gifts of I Corinthians 12 (which are given by the Holy Spirit as God chooses.) We cannot take a test to discover the gifts of the Spirit listed in Corinthians.

One of the very best teachings on the innate gifts that I have seen and helped me to discover my foundational gifts was put together by Marilyn Hickey. I would highly recommend the study of Romans 12 by her tapes and materials. It is important that these gifts in Romans 12 are not placed in the same category as the gifts of I Corinthians 12.

Most of the studies on how to find your gifts are not really Biblically accurate because they include the gifts of Corinthians and Romans. The gifts in Corinthians are given by the Holy Spirit and are not inborn. These gifts come and go as God chooses. We do not control where and when they are manifested. They come and go as people have needs.

There are other talents that people have at birth and can be developed. These gifts are needed in the church. Gifts related to music and leading worship etc. are wonderful talents and God is pleased when we use them for His glory but they are not a part of the list of Biblical gifts recorded in Romans or Corinthians. There are people who contribute greatly to the church by using their talents not mentioned in Scripture. Thank God for them. However one or more of the gifts listed in Romans 12 are found in every individual.

When we recognize our God given gifts and use them for the Kingdom of God we can see rich and sweet wine stored in a bottle and waiting to be poured out for God.

God created a variety of gifts for the benefit of mankind. Each of us has some gifts. Not all talents are listed as gifts in Scripture but we do find these gifts in people who are mentioned in Scripture. All gifts should bear some type of fruit when used for God's glory. We do however need to recognize that there are two particular passages in Scripture that name gifts. The ones described in Romans 12 are inborn and can be used or misused or ignored by every person. The ones in I Corinthians 12 are not controlled by people but by God and He gives as He sees they are needed and as we are open to allow the Holy Spirit to work them through us. These gifts bring forth fruit in our lives.

It is interesting to note that wine was used in Jewish offerings and worship. Wine comes from the fruit but is technically produced from the Vine. In fact wine is often called the fruit of the vine. Jesus is the Vine and I believe that was why God instructed the use of wine in the Jewish laws. The Jews were forbidden to drink blood, but they could have been told to use another type of fruit juice, but God chose wine. This was because it best represented the blood that would eventually come from the Vine when Jesus died on the cross. We use wine for communion today but just as it doesn't really matter what kind of bread we use to symbolize Christ's body I don't think it is wrong to use another type of juice for we have experienced His blood and body inwardly today, and the elements are only symbols of a finished work. In the Old Testament they were symbolic of a coming work and I feel needed to be more definite. I would like to add that I think it is good for us to use wine and unleavened bread as a more accurate symbol, but we should not get all bent out of shape and act unloving when we are using other types of things for the elements. After all they are still only symbols of what we have experienced personally.

Think about it

1. What Romans 12 gift(s) do you think you have been given?

2. Are you using your gift(s) in a way pleasing to God?

3. How are the I Corinthians 12 gifts different from those of Romans 12?

4. Does God want all Christians to be available to operate in the gifts of the Spirit (I Cor. 12)? Or just special leaders?

5. How do you feel about the choice/type of the elements for communion?

Chapter 19

Bottles and Wineskins

My sister and I have always enjoyed going to auctions. We like to look at old things and reminisce about our childhood and look at things we use to have and use when we were children in the 1940's. Once in a while we are so enthralled with an old item that we bid on it and hope to obtain it for a price we are willing to pay. For a number of years I collected all kinds of old bottles. These were old empty medicine bottles and long gone brands of liquid cleaning supplies and food products. I even had an old oil bottle with a metal cap that was used for car oil before tin cans were used. However as we get older we are trying to get rid of "stuff" and I have only a few special ones left on display. I still have a few different colored and shaped bottles from my time in Zimbabwe that I enjoy looking at from time to time.

Wine comes in many different sizes, styles, shapes and colors of bottles. I am not sure just what the significance of the kind of bottle has to do with the type of wine, or if there is any reason behind the kind of bottle. They are interesting to look at when I see them on display some place.

As Christians we have our wine in various physical sizes, styles, shapes and colors. We each have our own flavor depending on our circumstances and experiences. Something we need to remember is that you can not necessarily judge the quality of wine by the bottle. It is very easy to come to a wrong conclusion. We gather in a group of Christians and make critical observations of the containers. He/she cannot be a Christian because their "bottle" smells like smoke, or she

155

is not a good wine because her label isn't modest. That must be a low class cheap wine because the label looks ragged. There are tattoos on that bottle, so we better not invite him into our church. We might even see two of the same kind of bottles coming in to our church together but we don't want "those kinds" on our church "shelves." It is wrong to judge by exterior appearances. It is also wrong to ignore people who need Jesus simply because we do not like their appearance.

As Christians we are suppose to be producing grapes pleasing to God. We all go through different experiences and we may see our fruit in the form of table grapes, wine or raisins. Each type has its own unique packaging. There is one thing in common. We all have a container and we should not judge one another by looking only at the container.

One time while I was attending Messiah College I went home for the weekend with a friend. We went to her church on Sunday morning. When we got into her Sunday School class the teacher welcomed her and her friends home from college, but then went on to talk about the evils of higher education. He pointed out that when we get educated we lose our faith and depend on logic and reason, not God. I am not sure why he felt this way. He was judging our inner "wine" by our outward appearance of educated college students.

Sometimes we are not sure what it is about our exterior that makes us unacceptable. People have preferences and prejudices about our exterior "bottles." Another time I was at church and went into the sanctuary for the morning service. I had been attending that church for a while and knew almost everybody. I was a few minutes late for the service because I had taught a Sunday School class and one of the students wanted to ask a few questions, so I tried to quietly enter. The sanctuary was quite full but I saw a partially empty bench about halfway back from the front. There was just one couple sitting at one end so I started to sit down. The man slid over to me and informed me that the whole bench was saved. I went out feeling embarrassed and confused. I was not sure where I was going to find a place to sit. I went out and stood in a room that was behind the sanctuary so I could look for a place to sit. After a few minutes several children came in and sat down, leaving plenty of room for one more. No one else sat there. I did not understand why they felt there was not room for me. Somehow I did not seem to be the right bottle for that "shelf." Maybe they were hoping for a better more expensive looking bottle. I am not sure. I wondered if they would have treated a visitor the same way.

There are many vineyards which produce grapes for eating, but statistics show that about 80 per cent of the grape harvest is used for wine. As Christians we have the "wine" of the Holy Spirit in our earthly containers. We have "...this treasure in earthen vessels." The treasure is according to II Corinthians 4:7- the "light of the knowledge of the glory of God in the face of Jesus Christ." which is revealed knowledge that comes to us through the Holy Spirit.

Today wine is stored in various types of bottles, but in Biblical times wine was stored in wineskins. Jesus told a parable about putting new wine in old wineskins. The new wine refers to the Holy Spirit indwelling us. He desires to fill us the wine skins. However the wine of the Holy Spirit uses the grapes we are producing in our lives. He flows through humans to perform God's acts.

In chapter 14 we talked about the need for fasting to master our bodies. In Matthew 9 when Jesus was asked why His disciples did not fast He answered them by saying the day would come when they would and then He told the parable about the wineskins. He said wineskins would burst if new wine was put in them. In other words the Holy Spirit is powerful and we need to master our bodies or the Holy Spirit wine is limited in us because if we had the full power of the wine in uncontrolled flesh it would be destructive. We would burst. I think we have seen that happen in some well known Christian ministries. The very power of the Holy Spirit that desires to work through us to perform miracles is then in a wineskin not properly prepared and potential power in a flesh controlled Christian would be misused. We could use that power in a fleshly or carnal way and it would be manifested in anger or in unloving actions or reactions that are sinful and harmful. To produce the wine of the Holy Spirit we need a regenerated body and one that is obedient to our spirit and the Holy Spirit. How do we prepare our wineskins so that the flesh will not be in control?

Fasting makes the old wineskins new and capable of working under the power of the Holy Spirit. I believe that the reason we do not see more miracles and signs and wonders today is because the Spirit is not able to empower us with His wine. Christians are too flesh conscious. We are too self-centered and flesh focused or driven, for example our attitude on the road. If another driver pulled out in front of us we could respond in anger with destructive comments that could destroy that driver. We must be in control over our body and soul for God to entrust His children with this power of wine because if we misuse it, it will be an explosive bursting of wineskins. We can only produce the wine of the Holy Spirit in wineskins that are pure and constantly being worked on.

Our gifts of Romans and Corinthians must operate through pure wineskins in order to be used correctly for ministry in the church. If we attempt to use then on a flesh level the power of the Holy Spirit can cause us to "burst." God's gifts are powerful and if misused they can become destructive to others and to the person misusing them.

Sometimes when Christians first begin to use their gifts they will make mistakes because they are not yet mature in knowing how to use them. Their enthusiasm and excitement over being used by the Spirit and their love and compassion can cause them to run ahead of God and not wait for the proper timing. This is not the same as a Christian knowingly using a gift for selfish carnal purposes. We need to help one another and encourage each other in the proper use and correct time and place for the gifts to be manifested. That is why it is important to have spirit filled leaders in the church.

The gifts, especially the gifts, of the Spirit are not manifested in many churches because the leaders are not Spirit filled or do not operate in the gifts. In other churches the leaders fear the gifts or even deny they still exist. As a result they do not even teach them and refuse to let them be practiced. People using the gifts can make mistakes because they are human and not fully grown, but we all need to allow God to teach us how to mature. If we work together as a pastor and church God will fill our wine bottles with His spirit and will demonstrate His power and love toward people through the gifts.

We need to understand that God looks on the heart of man not on the outward appearance. We must not judge Christian people by their outer container. Neither should we criticize or shun unsaved people who might not have attractive "bottles" but we need to look into their hearts and help them to see Jesus can change them. Then we need to be sure we keep our own wineskin pure and allow the Spirit to use us for God's glory according to the plan and purpose He had in creating us.

Think about it

1. Do you judge the value of a person by outward appearances? Do your church people as a whole, judge by appearances?

2. How do you feel about people who are gay coming to your church? What about those with tattoos, rings in their body, etc?

3. How did Jesus treat and interact with the lower classes of people?

4. If your church is intolerant of certain groups of people what can you do to help them?

5. Have you ever been treated unkindly in a Christian church? How did you respond? If you are willing, share that experience.

Chapter 20

Raisins are Fruit

Our sociology/psychology teacher at Messiah College had a number of favorite maxims that he liked to repeatedly use to educate his students to the reality of life. They were good practical statements and I remember most of them. One of these was "the only thing that is constant is change." I have discovered that that is very true. I don't think change bothered me very much when I was twenty but I do find that as I get older change is not as easy as it use to be.

Although in some countries today a head of white hair is a sign to younger people that they must show respect and consideration, that is not true everywhere. In the more technologically advanced nations white hair or being old is a sign of being outdated and ignorant. This is probably the truth in many instances, because it is not easy to keep up with the fast moving technology of today's world. Technology is moving at such a rapid rate that when I enter the electronics department or store I feel like I have just been transplanted or maybe I should say "beamed up" into Star Wars!

Even though some of us are lacking in "know how" when it comes to technology, older people do have a lot of common sense and wisdom about living.

Also getting older does not mean we are no longer productive. We may retire from our vocation or career but that does not mean we retire from life. We might feel it is time to let some younger people begin to take over some of our jobs or church responsibilities, but it might be necessary that we gradually train them while we are still around. They will naturally have a lot of ideas of their own but they can learn some "old tricks" from a person who has had experience. These days many businesses and companies are beginning to see the value of older workers.

There is no record in Scripture about anyone reaching a particular age and retiring on a fixed income. Many people over the age of usual retirement are still very productive. Even a grapevine is able to produce fruit anywhere from 80 to 100 years. Should we quit at 65 or less?

I am reminded that God used many old people. Think about Moses, Abraham and Sarah, Caleb and Anna. God knows how many hairs on our heads and even how many we have lost, but I don't think He is counting how many birthdays we have had so He can let us go sit in a rocking chair and rock our last days away.

In Isaiah God gave a great promise to us when we get older:

> "And even to your old age I am He, and even to hoar hairs will I carry you; I have made, and I will bear; even I will carry, and deliver you." (Is. 46:4)

He also promises us that if we remain faithful to Him:

> "The hoary head is a crown of glory, **if** it be found in the way of righteousness." (Prov. 16:13)

Being in my 70's, that is a challenge to me. I want to let God use me up until the day He takes me home. There is a place and use for older grapes or "raisins."

Although we might think of raisins as old dried up grapes, I like to think of them as fully matured grapes which can be very useful. They are healthy snacks and add sweetness and nutrients to our diet. They are often added to bakery items, which gives some greater value and excuse for eating cookies and other baked goods!

As we get chronologically older we might discover our fruit changes. We need to be sure that we are still producing grapes even if they will be used as raisins. Talking from personal experience we find as we get older we can become more set in our ways and look at the younger generations as a bit hopeless in thinking and actions. It becomes easy to whine and complain about what the world and the church are coming to. But God expects raisins - sweeter and more mature grapes - to be an example and encouragement to the younger Christians. I can remember as a young person hearing the older church people complaining about us. We were less spiritual, more caught up in the world and ignorant of the church traditions. Now all of a sudden I am that older generation, and I do not want to be like that. I sometimes wonder if Joshua and Caleb had that feeling about the next generation. They were forced to live in the wilderness for forty years to wait for their generation to die. Did they see it as a blessing from God? Did they have ill will toward the older folks that were afraid to trust God and move into the Promised Land or did they see the next generation even more hopeless and less qualified to conquer the enemies? We don't really know, but at least there is no record of their complaining.

Joshua stayed open to the Lord's will and did some amazing things in his older years. When he finally got into his position of leadership we find him being used by God. The Lord did the supernatural through him-dividing the Jordan River, bringing down the walls of Jericho and dethroning thirty-one heathen kings to subdue a large portion of the Promised Land. Only once do we read that Joshua complained to the Lord and that was after Israel's defeat at Ai. "...O Lord God, wherefore hast thou at all brought this people over Jordan, to deliver us into the hand of the Amorites to destroy us? Would to God we had been content, and dwelt on the other side of Jordan." (Josh. 7:7) He whined a bit more until the Lord told him to get up and the Lord explained the reason for the defeat.

Although Scripture does not tell us more about Joshua's conversation with God, I think he might have felt embarrassed by jumping to the wrong conclusion about God and the lost battle. It is a reminder to us as we get older that we need to beware jumping to conclusions. It isn't only the young that jump to conclusions, even though they might be able to jump higher!

It is a challenge for us as we grow chronologically older and become senior citizens to watch and pray instead of criticize and grumble about the young people and the church going downhill. We have a responsibility to also encourage and teach the next generation both by words and example. We can teach them our traditions and music but teach it as tradition not Biblical command and be open to learn to worship with their style of music. We need to accept changes that do not compromise the Word of God. As we get older we should become more intimate with the Lord and love the Word more. We need to keep our relationship with God fresh and up-to-date. It is possible to have an up-to-date testimony to give and not always go back twenty or thirty years to some wonderful experience we had with the Lord.

As we get older are we becoming sweeter like raisins?

We should be gradually moving from the driver's seat to the backseat. Although we may retire from a particular job or career we are never instructed to retire from God's work. God can continue to use us and give us wisdom and strength to do ministry. The involvement might be in a different manner but we should still be involved. Our prayer should be "Cast me not off in the time of old age; forsake me not when my strength faileth." (Ps. 71:9) The Hebrew word for "strength" has a variety of meanings. It carries the idea of ability, physical force or even wealth. My strength may be less and my money more or less depending on my situation, but my ability and gifting are still with me. Even though I might not have some of the modern skills in certain areas like computers and technology, I still have a lot of practical experience and wisdom. God looks at His older children with delight, "The hoary head is a crown of glory, if it be found in the way of righteousness." (Pr. 16:31) The important thing to remember is that we must act in gentleness and with a heart open to change, not reacting with criticism and with the all too familiar words, "We never did it that way before" or "It will never work."

We must not be like the farmer who had spent his life working with horses. He could only find fault with the steam locomotive. He kept saying it will never work. When he finally saw one running the rails, he said, "It will not go as fast as my horses." Then when it did that he said, "It will never last. It's a passing fad." Attitudes like that do not produce raisins, in fact it wouldn't have ever produced tasty grapes, because it reflects a much deeper spiritual problem within me.

Since starting this book about vines and vineyards, I have found numerous verses in which God compared Israel to grapevines. We Christians should learn from God's illustrations to Israel. We are the descendants of Abraham and have been engrafted into the Jewish vine. We need to individually know God's Word and walk in all the truth He has for us. We need to beware false teaching, but cannot afford to miss our opportunities or ignore our giftings. The Holy Spirit within us can help us to continue to produce abundant fruit and to be sensitive to the leading of the Holy Spirit and open to His gifts.

The priests in Old Testament days, whether young or old, wore their prescribed vestments which had pomegranates and bells sewn to the hem. The pomegranates represented the fruit of our spirits representing God's character and the bells represented the gifts which the Holy Spirit manifests through us. So whether we are young, middle age or old Christians we are called God's priests and we should reflect the character of God and be available to the Holy Spirit to use in the gifts.

God warned us against false teachings and hindrances to producing an abundant harvest for Him. We must not degenerate into a wild vine:

> "I had planted you a choice vine, wholly of pure seed. How then have you turned into degenerate shoots of wild vine alien to me?" (Jeremiah 2:21) Amp.

Think about it

1. Do you complain about life today? Why? What do you see about the younger generation that you like or dislike?

2. How can you help the generation that will come after you? What are you doing now to help them?

3. The youth are leaving our churches. Why do you think they are? How can we keep our youth?

4. Do you have trouble making changes? In what areas? How can you improve your attitude?

Chapter 21

No Fruitful Branches in the Wilderness

It is interesting to me to watch people in their work habits. While living in Zimbabwe we had a fellow missionary who was really very talented. He could fix anything from the bell system at the school to motorcycles and watches. He was good at directing the workmen in building new classrooms when needed at the school. Besides all that he taught Science to the high school students. What was so interesting to me was the fact that he could have a dozen different projects going on at the same time and manage to keep his wits about him. Today we use the term multi-tasking. He was able to move from one thing to another.

That is not me. I start one project and don't like stopping and starting a dozen different times. When I start a project I like to keep at it until it's done and if I don't think I can finish it in a few hours I just avoid doing it. I hate starting something I can't complete. Perhaps that is why this book has taken me so long to write. I have had to work at it in bits and pieces over a long time and that is difficult for me. I prefer doing one task and working on it until it is finished. Then I can go on to the next job. I do not multi-task well. I think it is because it takes me a long time to get started on some tasks, but once I get going I want to get it done. Interruptions are an annoyance to me but a very real part of my life.

Everybody is different than everybody else, but that is how God made us. We need all kinds of work styles for all kinds of jobs.

The style of our work habits isn't the important thing as long as we keep working and moving forward to complete the task. What is sad is to see those who just quit and never move on at all. They simply stop because they lose interest or caring. How many great inventions, works of art, projects never were finished? How do people lose their steam and dream? Some of these tasks were actually God-given or ordained by God?

There was a whole generation of Israelites that never finished the task God had for them- to get to the Promised Land. How sad that Samson allowed his flesh to overrule all God might have had for him to do. The Rich Young Ruler missed God's plan for his life. How many other people have missed their true calling and spent their life working diligently at the wrong task? I have talked to some individuals who admitted in their older years that they missed God's best. They always have good reasons (?) for their choices and I know they did some things for God, but they missed the abundant fruitful life that God designed for them. They took second best.

The Vine was always with them even though He had not yet been made manifest physically. Yet they wasted forty years in the wilderness missing God's best. A whole generation died without enjoying the fruit God had waiting for them. There were no grapes in the wilderness. There were no grapes because there were no fruitful branches. The Israelites did not produce or eat grapes for forty years in the wilderness. The last grapes they must have seen (and possibly eaten) were when they were camped in Kadesh-Barnea and the twelve spies went out to search the land and they brought back a cluster of grapes so large in size that it had to be brought back by two men carrying it on a staff. It would seem that the idea of moving into a land so fruitful plus God's mighty works of bringing them out of Egypt should have urged them to move on to conquer the Promised Land, but because of their fear of the Anakim and their lack of faith in the God of the impossible, they were destined to miss their dream for the abundant life and remain unfruitful until they died. They heard only the words of the ten spies, "...we were in our own sight as grasshoppers..." (Nu. 13:20) They focused on their own limited ability instead of Jehovah God's power.

They never partook of the vineyards' bountiful harvest and the abundant life that God had planned for them. I wonder if during those forty years their thoughts went back to that cluster of grapes and they regretted their unbelief.

How sad it is that in the church today there are many who never go on to enjoy all the promises of God. They never reach the Promised Land. They are released from the bondage of Egypt but spend their life wandering in the wilderness. While there God meets their needs but they do not experience the abundant life.

Many Christians today say that the Promised Land or Canaan is symbolic of heaven. In fact songs have been written about Canaanland as heaven, but Canaan is not a symbol of heaven. There were enemies and battles to fight in Canaan. There were opportunities to be disobedient and to sin. That does not symbolize heaven in my mind. So what does the Promised Land represent?

As I see this journey for human beings from Egypt to the land of Canaan this is what it symbolizes. Egypt is the unsaved state of man who is born in sin. It is bondage. Christ died to redeem man from bondage and when man accepts salvation he is released from Egypt (bondage) and enters the journey through the wilderness. This is the state of being born again. God moves us to the Red Sea with the promise of Canaan. That is the journey for the Christian when they are growing but realize they are missing something. We can cross the Red Sea into the Promised Land which is the baptism of the Holy Spirit. The journey through the wilderness into the Spirit filled life can be a very short period of time, but many wander about for years before understanding this second encounter with the Holy Spirit. Some actually die without ever having come to the abundant fruitful life.

Some do choose to enter that Promised Land and experience new power from being placed into the Spirit. They are able to operate fully in the gifts explained in I Corinthians 12. There are still enemies but new gifts and authority which enable them to conquer. In Canaan Christians are more fully equipped to defeat their enemies. However, many Christians die in the wilderness without ever experiencing the Promised Land. Entire denominations and churches die in the wilderness because of their failure to believe in the baptism of the Holy Spirit and as a result never teach it to their members. They are saved and on their way to heaven but never have the power of a prayer language or the gifts. They are described by Paul:

"Having a form of godliness, but denying the power thereof..." (II Tim. 3:5)

The word for "form" carries the idea of a **"trace."** The word **"godliness"** means being like God, or having the character of God. In other words that verse states that there are Christians who have a **trace** of the character of God. Are they saved? I am sure they are, but they only have a trace of what God is like. They see God in His love, grace and mercy that saves them but miss the creative miracle working power of the character of God that desires to do miracles and wonderful things for His children. God is powerful. He performs miracles. He heals and reveals. We can have these same attributes working in us on a human level, because we are created in His image!

Jesus illustrated this fruitful life when He ministered on earth. We are to be like Him. Jesus still has the power to work miracles and give signs and wonders through us, because He lives in us and Jesus is the "same yesterday, today, and forever." He has made these gifts available to us if we just choose to enter into this abundant fruitful life. It is available in spite of those who tell us these things passed away somewhere back in history. They can't point to a specific place or time when this happened but they somehow imagine that God took these wonderful gifts away from His Children or that they got lost somewhere in the building of the church or maybe just gradually faded away. We at times say ignorance is bliss but in regard to the gifts that is surely an incorrect statement.

Why would anyone not want to receive the fullness of God's Spirit and power in his life? We need only ask and believe we receive and then walk in that fullness of the Promised Land. In Canaan we will receive fuller revelation and operate in words of wisdom, knowledge and gifts of faith, healing, miracles, prophecy, discernment and tongues for personal edification and public edification. God is calling His church to a new time and day to build a church and to reach the world. This is the empowered church that will fulfill and characterize the End Times. This will be a church producing an abundant harvest of grapes, wine and raisins because of their intimate abiding in Christ the Vine. Where do we fit in this picture? I want to be a vital part of God's kingdom. What about you?

Someone once said, "If you always do what you have always done, you will always be what you have always been." The choice is yours and mine to make. Will we end that vicious cycle? Remember these things:

The baptism of the Spirit is Biblical and you can receive it with the evidence of speaking in tongues.

Find someone with whom you can share your experience and be accountable to them.

Realize growth takes time but praying in your prayer language will aid maturing.

Know that satan will attack and try to convince you that nothing happened to you and your prayer language is all emotional gibberish.

Keep praising God in your prayer language and in your natural language.

Remember you are still human and you will be tempted but if you sin you can go to God and ask for His forgiveness.

Last of all realize that maturing and producing "grapes" takes time but we don't have to work at the producing part. We work at the abiding and fellowshipping with God and Christ.

Jesus said, "I am the vine, ye are the branches. He that abideth in me, and I in him, the same bringeth forth much fruit..." (Jn. 15:5)

Think about it

1. What is life like for a person who chooses second best?

2. What is your dream or purpose that God has given you?

3. What hinders you from fulfilling that purpose?

4. How does God enable you to do that work?

5. What regrets do you already have and how can you change that?

Chapter 22

Vines Were Created to Give

God created the heavens and earth. We read in Psalm 24:1-"The earth is the Lord's, and the fulness thereof; the world, and they that dwell therein." After sin entered the world, satan was called the "prince of the world." (Jn. 12:31)

Although Jesus destroyed satan's authority in the world, he continues to deceive and control men to do his (satan's) purpose through the world's systems. satan is a taker. God is a giver. God desires to give and bless us. satan comes to steal, kill and destroy. (Jn. 10:10) So now we have a choice to be like God and be a giver or listen to satan's voice and be a taker. In the beginning the natural world was a giver, but after it was corrupted and cursed because of sin it changed. It now gives but also takes. Some living things only take from others and produce nothing good. Some living things still give and produce benefits or fruit. Grape vines function that way. They were created to produce fruit.

Adam and Eve were created to be givers but also because of their being human flesh they had to take from creation. They were created in God's image and so were a perfect balance of spirit, soul and flesh. Sin changed that whole nature of man so that today we are born with a sinful nature. We are still created by God and in the image of God. At conception God gives us gifts, talents and abilities so we can bless others, but unlike the plant and animal kingdom, man has a choice in being a giver or a taker.

We are born with a sin nature which creates in us a "taker" personality. Children are born selfish. It doesn't take long to learn that even a baby wants its own way. Parents need to **teach** children to **be givers**. As Christians we need God's love to fill us so that we want to give and enjoy giving. We need to give of our time, gifts, talents and (yes)our money. It might be easier to give of our gifts and talents because they are noticed by others and it makes our soul and flesh "feel" good, but sometimes it is very hard to give of our time and money if no one notices.

In Zimbabwe the Christians did not have a lot of money. Yet in other ways they were very generous. If you visited them in their villages they were sure to give you something- eggs or a chicken or some homegrown or homemade item. However when you talked to them about giving money or offerings to the Lord through the church they had more difficulty.

An African Christian woman asked a missionary an unusual question. "What is better- to give a penny willingly or to give a shilling (dime) grudgingly?" It might be easy to smile at her question but what about us? Can we give a tithe willingly? Can we even give of our time willingly? Although I don't know of any Bible verse that directly talks about giving of our time willingly, we are given instructions about our responsibilities for others- to encourage, to help, to bear, to warn, to teach, etc. These take our time!

When the missionary told me the story about the African that asked her about giving a little willingly or to give more but to do it grudgingly, I remember what I thought. Perhaps the missionary should have asked the same question. What is there in me that I cannot always give whatever the Lord asks of me willingly? When the topic of money and giving comes up we can get a bit tense, so let me add a little humor to this topic - the Lord loves a cheerful giver, but accepts from a grouch!

This really isn't a book about giving. It's about having a fruitful life. If we are a branch connected to the True Vine we will be fruitful in every area of our lives. The more intimately we are abiding the easier it becomes to be a giver of all God has given us - time, talent and possessions. It is impossible to be fruitful and not include these three parts of our lives. Our fruit is seen in our actions and not just publicly so others know. We read the words of Jesus regarding giving in Matthew 6:3 - "let not thy left hand know what thy right hand doeth." This applies to the church today as it did to God's Chosen People, the Jews, in His day. We the church are a body. The left "hand" in the body does not need to know what I, as the right "hand", give. The same idea applies to our time and talents. At times the rest of the "body" will see or learn what we are doing but that should never be our purpose in giving or serving in the church.

Why and how do I give and serve in the Church? Is it because I am responding to the Vine and it just comes out or is it for praise or done as a duty?

So while we are thinking about money and being fruitful in our giving let me include a few thoughts on Biblical offerings. There are different kinds of offerings and types of giving mentioned in Scripture:

> Tithing - This is mentioned a number of times in the Bible. It is giving 10 per cent of your income to the "storehouse." (Mal. 3:8-10) Some teach that this is Old Testament. However Jesus said this about tithing- "ye ought to have done" it. If we don't like this concept think about the New Testament teaching of stewardship which means nothing is ours. It all belongs to God. Giving a tithe is the minimum. Our church should receive at least that amount.

> Offerings - This is above the tithe for other ministries or special needs in your church. (Luke 6:38)

> Alms - This is giving to the poor or ministries that help the poor and this might be someone you know or through some Christian organization, like Salvation Army, or a city mission that helps the poor and needy. (II Corinthians 9:6-12)

There are other special offerings and opportunities to give of our finances. As we learn to listen to the Lord, He will direct our giving.

I would suggest you read the three Scripture passage given and see the whole picture of the type of giving in context of the chapter. Also look to see that each of these has a reward that comes back to us when we become a giver. That does not mean you give to get. That defeats the whole purpose of giving, but it reminds us that God is also a giver and will reward you with His blessings when we give as He directs.

Giving of ourselves through time and talents is also a part of the stewardship teaching of Scripture.

Think about it

1. What answer would you give a person who asked about giving a penny cheerfully?

2. What is the problem with a person who doesn't enjoy giving?

3. What are the rewards/blessings that come from each type of giving?

Chapter 23

Some Grapes Have Seeds

In Zimbabwe we had a delicious fruit called a guava. It is about the size and color of a lemon, but has a smooth skin. The inside is red and it is soft like a peach and very sweet. The taste is unique but it is good. It is found here in the States these days- often as a mixture with other juices. I really liked guavas. There was one problem with eating them. They were full of little white seeds about the size of the head of a straight pin. You did not want to chew a guava because of the little hard seeds but you learned to just smash it in your mouth and swallow it. We often would cook them just a bit and put them through a sieve like making applesauce and that was the way I enjoyed it most- no seeds.

In America we have a variety of grapes and some have seeds. Concord grapes have seeds. I like the taste of concord grapes but I just swallow the inside with the seeds and enjoy the flavor of the juice. When I buy grapes I always look for the seedless variety because I really don't like biting down on a seed. Sometimes in our local store they will have both seedless and grapes with seeds on the same display table and I get the ones with seeds accidentally. I am always a bit disappointed when that happens. Grapes with seeds, like guavas, are still good, but a little less enjoyable when eaten because you never know when you will bite down on something hard.

Some Christians are like fruit with seeds and/or pits. In fact probably most of us have a few seeds hiding deep within us and while we might not be aware of them, others notice them. When we are with a fellow Christian something happens and suddenly you just discovered a seed. What are "seeds" in the Christian's life?

Scripture talks about "strongholds." These are personal beliefs, ideas, or opinions that we use to fortify, protect or defend what **we** believe about ourselves, someone else or even God. They are incorrect concepts or lies that were erected in our minds because of a personal bad experience or teaching. They are like seeds. They are not noticeable most of the time, but some event or circumstance occurs and we "feel the seed." satan sees that stronghold in us and loves to keep us thinking that way to deceive us in our thoughts and eventually our actions. He is so clever in this kind of deception that he can even convince us that the voice we are hearing is actually the voice of God. satan is a counterfeiter. satan tells us that because we have some messed up things in our life from the past or even present, and that our future will be affected. In fact he deceives us into thinking this stronghold thought is truth and is coming from God. But in reality it diminishes our relationship with God and others. Sometimes it makes us a crusader for a cause- right or wrong - that is not from God or is not our calling. It can take us Christians into a battle that was never meant for us to enter. This only opens us for more demonic attacks and deceptions.

Sometimes through our environment and circumstances our souls have been damaged by unhappy events that haunt us- some are own fault and some not. These experiences create strongholds or attitudes in our minds that are not true but that satan convinces us are true. This does not completely destroy our ministry for God or our fruitfulness, but puts limitations on us by putting "seeds" in our life that affect or even hurt others.

Wrong concepts of God that come from strongholds of past experiences, especially if we feel we did the wrong thing, limit us because we feel we are not worthy of God's help and blessings. However we need to remember that if we base the kind of blessings and benefits we receive from God on our worthiness we would never receive and enjoy any of God's goodness, because no matter how wonderful or good we have been it would never be enough to impress God so that He would be obligated to share His blessings and benefits with us.

How can we get rid of these strongholds in our life?

The first thing is to seek God to find out if we have any strongholds and then be willing to admit we have them. This can be done by spending time "praying in the spirit" and listening to God. Spend time in the Word and ask God to make it personal to you. He is eager to give you a "rhema" word. When past experiences and hurts come to your mind, refuse to dwell on them and replace those thoughts with God's Word, blessings and promises. Read II Corinthians 10:5. Secondly we can ask for the mind of Christ. (Phil. 2:5) Use the Biblical principle of binding and loosing- bind your mind to God and loose any strongholds. Do these things until you feel free from wrong attitudes.

If we do not deal with strongholds they can in time make us feel life is not worth living and we can open ourselves to a spirit of death or suicide. Even if it doesn't lead to that type of depression it will always limit the full power and authority of God from working through us.

There is no way we can remove past hurts from our memory or prevent future hurts from coming to us, but we can control how they affect us. We can allow God to use them to reach out to others and have compassion on those who are hurting.

When I was a child and someone said something nasty to me or about me, my mother would tell me to say this:

> "Sticks and stones may break my bones but names and words will never hurt me."

Better advice is found in God's Word:

> "'No weapon that is formed against thee shall prosper; and every tongue that shall rise against thee in judgment thou shalt condemn. This is the heritage of the servants of the Lord, and their righteousness is of me,' saith the Lord." (Is. 54:17)

No matter what my past hurts may be, whether self inflicted or caused by others, they can be forgiven by God and by me and I can produce "seedless" fruit. Also seeds reproduce and I will not reproduce my "seeds" of hurt into the generation that comes after me.

If we want to be free and be and do what God has designed for us to be and do, we need to recognize that they exist and reside in us and remove them:

> "...refute arguments and theories and reasonings and every proud and lofty thing that sets itself up against the true knowledge of God; lead every thought and purpose away captive into the obedience of Christ." (II Cor. 10:4) Amp.

Sometimes we might need special help because of very difficult circumstances which we have endured. There are good Christian books on this subject. One that has been a help to me is *Shattering Your Strongholds* by Liberty Savard. To admit to having strongholds in our lives is difficult but we need to realize many Christians have had or still have strongholds in their lives. God desires us to be free from any and all strongholds. This will make our personal lives better and also help us to serve the Lord with more freedom, power and authority.

Think about it

Perhaps this chapter is more personal and people would rather separate and spend their time with God not others. Talking about past issues with others can create tension and /or embarrassment. If some have questions you may be able to discuss them as a group or it might be best to have a one-on-one time.

N.B. Some types of strongholds may come from more serious hurts, e.g. physical or sexual abuse. When someone has these kinds of issues it is good to seek professional and Christian counseling.

A Modern Day Parable

There was a certain man who owned a large vineyard. He sent his vinedresser out to cultivate and prune the vine that it should bring forth an abundant harvest. Some branches needed much pruning and some needed only a little. The vinedresser began to prune them gently one by one. He knew what each branch needed to bring forth grapes.

Many of the branches submitted willingly to the sharp cutting because they knew the purpose was to help them bring forth more and sweeter fruit. Others complained that it hurt too much and it wasn't necessary. They pulled away from the hands of the vinedresser refusing to be pruned.

He trimmed away the tendrils of the vines that were not His. (Jer. 5:10)

In the spring the vinedresser went forth to feed and water the vine and branches. The pruned branches drank in the water and fed on the nutrients knowing it was good and would enable them to bring forth much fruit. Again some of the branches said they did not like that food and that much water was not necessary, so they refused to absorb the healthful feeding. Others said they were too busy trying to produce fruit and they didn't have time to take in nourishment. Some said they liked the old fertilizers better and refused to accept the new nutrients.

When the time of the reaping of the harvest came, the vinedresser arrived to glean the grapes, some for eating fresh and others to make wine. He left some there to make sweet raisins. However some branches had sour grapes, some had bitter grapes, some had few grapes and some had no grapes. But the branches that had allowed the hand of the vinedresser to care for them as he knew best brought forth a bountiful harvest - some an hundredfold, some sixty-fold, and some thirty-fold providing wholesome and sweet food and drink for the hungry and thirsty of the world.

Printed in the United States
By Bookmasters